The Angeles Arrien Foundation for Cross-Cultural
Education and Research Series

No. 2

The Mill House Speaks

Seven Pathways to the Ancestral Basque Homeland

Denise Orpustan-Love

Foreword by Angeles Arrien

Center for Basque Studies Press
University of Nevada, Reno

This book was published with the generous financial assistance of the Basque government and the Angeles Arrien Foundation for Cross-Cultural Education and Research

The William A. Douglass Center for Basque Studies
University of Nevada, Reno
www.basque.unr.edu/books

The Angeles Arrien Foundation for Cross-Cultural Education and Research Series, no.2

Copyright © 2017 Denise Orpustan-Love
Photos courtesy of Delaney Orpustan Love copyright © 2017

Book design by Daniel Montero

Library of Congress Control Number: 2017956364

For Beñat and Delaney — My Sun and Moon

Contents

Foreword	1
Angeles Arrien	
Preface	5
Acknowledgments	7
1. The Way of Wholeness	9
Lesson 1	31
2. The Way of the Ancestors	33
Lesson 2	43
3. The Way of the Home	45
Lesson 3	73
4. The Way of the Land	75
Lesson 4	97
5. The Way of the Village	99
Lesson 5	117
6. The Way of Two Worlds	121
Lesson 6	143
7. The Way of the Universe	145
Lesson 7	157
Appendix: Seven Pathways Integration	159
Endnotes	167
Bibliography	179

Foreword

> "The Earth is the center of the Universe.
> The House is the center of the Earth.
> The Family is the center of the House.
> The Person is the center of the Family."
> — Basque Song

The major Spiritual traditions of the world, all have their roots embedded in mysticism — the honoring of the mystery of life, land, place, home, family, ancestors; and the ritualized mysteries, of birth, initiation, marriage, and death. These are universal experiences, regardless of our cultural imprinting and family conditioning, and are time-honored values and perennial wisdoms shared by the human species.

Humans long for direction and guidance from their ancestral roots, as they search for meaning to the signs and omens on their own pilgrimage. The Seven Pathways, although rooted in Basque mysticism, reflect the universal mysticism of all people. These pathways decode the common mystical experiences of ancient cultures into an understandable, concrete, and practical map for navigating the complexities of today's modern world.

The Basques originally settled in the Pyrenees Mountains where they remain today in seven provinces — four located on the Spanish side of the Pyrenees, and three on the French side of the Pyrenees, off the Bay of Biscay. The Basque culture, including its origin and its language, remains a mystery today. Linguists have only been able to identify and confirm that the Basque language is not an Indo-European language in its origin; and that the Basques preceded Cro-Magnon man and the first Iberians. What is known is that Basques still govern themselves democratically; are committed to free enterprise; and remain economically self-sufficient through their fishing, farming, banking, manufacturing, and land-based cooperatives. The Seven Pathways, integrated by Denise Orpustan-Love, are both rooted and grounded in the simple, yet time-honored perennial wisdoms of ancient Basque people. These pathways still hold the inherent values and worldview embodied among Basque people today.

The Basques, like all people, have been faced with numerous challenging decisions — whether to stay on the farm, go to sea, be more urban, or sustain life both at home and abroad. Their ability to make everyday life and larger communal decisions, are based upon hidden, unspoken, and deeply sacred aspects of their culture. The pathways give people of today a sacred way of making meaning out of all the seemingly complex dimensions of life.

Even though this book is about the author's journey to understand her roots, ancestral heritage; and discovering her unexplainable longings and character qualities, her journey is a universal journey that each individual undertakes at some time in life. The Seven Pathways themselves, although deeply embodied and lived by Basques, will trigger deep associations for everyone in what is equally important in their own spiritual and ancestral journey, especially during times of deep change and transition.

When faced with change, choice, challenge or crossroads, the pathways offer guidance, both in understanding the influence of the past, and embracing with courage and strength, the opportunities of the future. The Seven Pathways give direction to life's journey. They help to make sense of daily decisions that follow the sun and moon; monthly or yearly seasonal cycles, and even lifelong patterns, by restoring balance. When one pathway is missing or diminished, simple decisions may be difficult or the direction of one's life may be off course. Today's complex and overloaded informational, technological and materialistic age, has left humans scrambling for direction and meaning. The return to the simple life often seems idealistic and unattainable; yet the pathways give everyone a way of accessing universal spiritual wisdoms for the simplest, or most complicated, of life's choices.

Denise Orpustan-Love's journey is a universal journey experienced by men and women worldwide. There is not a culture in the world that does not honor the ancestors; or does not cherish the deep human values inherent in The Seven Pathways. The Basque philosopher Miguel Unamuno in his book, *The Tragic Sense of Life*, reminds us of the importance of ancestral connections and the help that is deeply rooted within us, "All my ancestors live undiminished in me and will continue to live, united with me, in my descendants." The path of remembrance is right in front of all of us, often so obvious we are blinded by it. The Seven Pathways are just that; obvious yet often overlooked. By integrating each of the pathways into everyday life, we see that each moment is sacred and purposeful. Each encounter, however mundane or magical, is part of the larger path we all share. Denise Orpustan-Love offers a timely and invaluable resource that not only honors the ancestors, but brings alive the world's perennial wisdoms to guide present and future generations.

— *Angeles Arrien, Cultural Anthropologist*
(whose Basque maternal and paternal heritage
precedes the fifteenth century)

Preface

"The House is our sun"
— Michael Duvert, 1994

The house is life for the Basques. The Basque house (*etxe*) is the center of family and community life in the Basque Country. The Mill House, a eighteenth-century old mill passed down to me by my Basque immigrant father, is more than stones, brick, and mortar. The *etxe* is sacred. It is the name of the house that prevails over all those who have lived or live in it. The *etxe* is fully integrated with all aspects of life and death and is in constant relation with nature and the earth, and in communication with ancestor spirits. The ancient Basques believed that the *etxe* was connected to the upper world, the stars, sky (heavens), sun, moon, thunder, lightning, and plants, as well as to the underworld, the place where the ancestors' spirits lived. These spirits communicated through particular points of entry, routes or pathways within the house. Both worlds, the upper physical world (daily activities) and the lower under world (spirituality), were intertwined, inseparable, and united as one.

The Mill House Speaks is a remarkable story about the journey of returning to my father's ancestral homeland in the Basque Country in the summer of 2015 with my children, following the passing of my beloved mentor, cultural anthropologist Angeles Arrien, Ph.D. In honoring the promise I made to her to do a project on Basque folklore, I honestly, candidly, and courageously share this journey. In this research trip to my father's homeland in the Basque Country, I discovered that the "project" is much more than a collection of literature on ancient Basque folklore, but an ancestral journey of living folklore, tied to my father's sacred mill house.

The Mill House Speaks integrates our daily synchronistic experiences on this summer research trip to the Basque Country in France. *The Mill House Speaks* describes in detail the life dreams of rebuilding Papa's mill house and creating a project on Basque folklore with my mentor. Through daily observations, experiences, and storytelling in the village of my father, I reflect on the road that brought me here. Supported by literature on ancient Basque folklore and ethnographic research, I discover that all parts of the journey, the present and past, are united as one, just like the ancient *etxe*.

The seven pathways are the integrated aspects of this journey, reflecting the parts of the ancient Basque world and belief system. The seven pathways are a synthesis of this ancient Basque world, all connected to the major areas of life, including life lessons from nature and perennial wisdoms, daily life actions (sun), inner qualities/character attributes (moon), the cycles of the seasons, and everyday tools for building one's life dream.

In its entirety, *The Mill House Speaks* is a guided journey of *living folklore*, both memoir and storytelling, for my children and future generations, to pass on the enduring wisdoms of the human spirit.

Acknowledgments

I am forever grateful for all those who have helped me write this book, especially:

For my mentor Angeles Arrien, my father Bernard (Beñat) Orpustan, my mother Ann Orpustan, and all my ancestors for your continual blessings, guidance, inspiration, wisdom, and unconditional love. I share this book with all of you.

For the generous legacy grant from the Angeles Arrien Foundation for Cross-Cultural Education and Research, and the fiscal administration from the Basque Educational Organization (BEO) in San Francisco, California.

For my family and friends in the Basque Country for always opening your homes and hearts to my family and I. I cherish your trust, loyalty, friendship, and love.

For my devoted and loving husband Chad Love, for standing by my side every step of the way.

For my daughter, Delaney Orpustan Love, for her beautiful photographs.

For all those from the Center for Basque Studies (CBS) Press at the University of Nevada Reno, and especially to

Sandra Ott for her support of this work, and Daniel Montero for his excellent editing and design of this book.

1
The Way of Wholeness

> *"Nothing is lost, nothing wholly passes away, for in some way or another everything is perpetuated; and everything, after passing through time, returns to eternity"*
> — Miguel de Unamuno, Basque philosopher

Saturday, June 6, 2015

Looking out at the planes on the runway preparing for take-off at the Dublin Airport, Beñat, twelve, thin, tall, with deep blue eyes, brown hair, and protruding Basque ears, sits to my right and Delaney, just fifteen the day before, a tall, beautiful blond California girl, smiling in wonder at all the planes taking off, grips my hand to my left. I'm always in the middle of my two children on this trip to avoid teenage confrontations. There are no smartphones or laptops to distract us. There's nothing to do but wait for the Ryan Air flight attendant to call our flight number. Knowing I will see my family in a few hours, I realize it is now the moment to tell the children exactly why we are here and who we will be possibly meeting at the airport in Biarritz. I feel the brewing thunder of emotions in my belly, finding the inner strength and power to tell the children, once again, the story of Angeles, Papa, and the Mill House.

Waterfall on Arzamendi, Bidarrai

I remind Delaney and Beñat that this trip would not have been possible without Angeles. Although they never met her, they certainly know her by name. My daughter thinks it's even more special that she doesn't know what she looks like, because she feels the presence of her spirit. I have been talking about our connection for their entire lives. Every month for a year after her passing, I lit a special candle on my ancestor shrine at our home in California at her request.

The offerings of light are the highest honor for the ancestors. Light offerings are a type of payment or *ordain*. The women lead these ancient rituals of light, where "the wax candle represents the body; the light is an image of the spirit that gives it life." Lighting candles is associated with helping ancestor spirits to transition into the spirit world, but also as magic rituals to ward off evil spirits or illness, or prevent harm, such as thievery to someone in the village. The ancient Basques attributed magical events, associated with lighting wax candles to a force called *adur,* the connection between an object and its image or representation.

> *Of the offerings made to the dead, the offering of light is the most important.*

An example of *adur* is the story of a Ataun resident who consulted with an *azti* (seer) from Tolosa after his cow was stolen. The seer advised the man to light a candle to represent the thief. The thief would then waste away as the candle gradually burned down.

I tell my children that in Lower Navarre, the province where our village Ortzaize (Ossès in French) is located, the bereaved then return to the home before an illuminated fire before the door, all in a circle, where the people remain in contemplation. The meal (*l'eskaratze*), is planned by the village carpenter who makes the provides the bread, wine, and eventually coffee. In effect, the meal may be modest but has the appearance of a true banquet. The prayer begins by the cantor, first neighbor, or even the priest if he is invited . One can address the deceased only by the name of their house (*atera diren arimentzat,* for the souls that have departed). These rituals all take place within the house, a cycle that comes full circle.

In ancient times, the first periods of formal bereavement was organized by the ceremonies of women. The mourning officially opened at the end of the funeral procession, where the woman closest to the dead (if it is a woman who has died) is followed by her first neighbor, who carries a basket of waxes of mourning (*ezkoak*). For this occasion, she receives the title of *argizaina* (guardian of light). There is first a formal year of mourning, where the domestic group of the deceased places four *kandelak* (candles) on the table supporting the coffin during the church burial service. These *kandelak* refer to the household *sépulture* or *yarleku* (family site within the church that is connected to the family tombstone in the graveyard) that are used during the year of mourning. The *sépulture* is central to the formal mourning cycle. During the year of formal mourning, the female members of the domestic group have an obligation to attend Sunday High Mass and High Masses on all religious holidays in order to activate the *sépulture* by the lighting the *kandelak*.

It is felt that the members of the bereaved domestic group should observe a period of intense personal mourning, lasting about eighteen months, followed by a six-month period of half mourning. For the initial mourning during that first year, dress restrictions and social withdrawal are fully observed. The period of half mourning is more relaxed and constitutes a transitional state between bereavement and the resumption of normal activities.

It is quite common to celebrate memorial or anniversary masses (*memorizhek*) for a number of years after a death. I remind the children how I still light a candle in our house every December 23 for Papa for his *memorizhek*. Since he is not buried in the cemetery and has no *sépulture*, this ritual seems even more important. During ancient times, these rituals were very specific. The priests are informed and a date is set; the impending celebration is announced from the pulpit. On the day of the service the *etxekoandre* (married female head-of-household) places her *kandelak* on the household *sépulture*. In addition, close relatives and a few neighbors who perceive a social obligation will also place a *kandela* on the *sépulture* of the deceased. However, if one spouse dies at a relatively young age, the other may offer yearly *memorizhek* until his or her own death, as I have done, since Papa was only thirty-one when he died. In any event, with the passing years, participation on the part of relatives and neighbors tends to decline. Ultimately, it becomes solely a domestic group affair, and it eventually terminates altogether. There also existed the masses of neighbors. These ceremonies have now become less frequent, but the classic mass at the end of the year (*urte buruko meza*) still exists.

As I recount this history to the children, a distinct, vivid memory flashes in front of me. I begin to tell the children, "My aunt and Godmother Marie Jeanne, the matriarch of the family (*etxekoandre*), is standing over me at the dining room table at Irochbeheria, the name of the *baserri* (family farm house) where Papa was born. *Etxe* are named and people in the village are identified by its name, an ancient Basque tradition. Even today, the women are still very much the center of the house and its domestic life. In the Middle Ages, the mistress of the house was responsible for all the activities of social and religious life. For centuries, women in the old country were given great responsibility in the Catholic Church, as they were once the priestesses and healers. The mistress of the house was responsible for the rituals of the house and of the church. The family mother family blessed the house and her children once in the springtime, protected the hearth and fire in ceremonies, and cared for the domestic animals. Today, the women are still very much the center of the house and domestic life: the etxekoandre maintains a strong sense of responsibility for the rituals of the house, giving her strength and power. A folk belief held by many people still exists about the power, or perhaps loving control, that many women seem to have in their family house.

I go on to describe how my aunt, this tall, thin and muscular woman, whom I've never seen sit down except to eat and sleep, holds on to the corners of that long thick wooden table, that wooden table that is the center of their home and social life, similar to our front room-that table that has heard the stories of generations of family. My strong and fiercely Basque aunt carefully places a piece of paper in front of me, with much forethought and precision. As the matriarch of the house, she has inherited this role when the *baserri* was passed down to her. The house is traditionally passed down to the first born, either male or female (*premu* or *alaba gehiena*) but my uncle, the first born, pursued an academic career as a university professor, while my aunt and her husband took over the *baserri*. My father, not having a place in the village or on the farm anymore, emigrated to America. Like many other Basques during that major migration to the American West in the early- to mid-1900s, they came without much more than the clothes on their back. They were young and strong and willing to work for a chance in life they couldn't have in the old country. They entered the American West as sheepherders. It was a harsh, solitary, lonely, and rugged life that required an immovable strength of spirit, courage, and tenacity.

Although my children only know me as their middle-aged mother, I explain to them that I too had a pioneering spirit of my own, just twenty-three years old, having decided to fly *toute seul* (completely alone) to the Basque Country for the summer for no reason except I couldn't answer the "why not" question: why not leave? I had just ended a five-year relationship. I was in between my first and second year as a graduate student in social work at UC Berkeley, and a Basque cousin by marriage had left her home in San Francisco to do the same. I couldn't think of any reason not to go to the Basque Country, so I bought the ticket and flew away.

I continue with the story of my aunt, "I felt so far away from the world I had always known in California but at the same time, sitting at the long oak table at Irochbeheria, I felt more at-home than I ever felt in my entire life. Marie Jeanne is leaning over me, smelling of bacon grease, wearing a kitchen towel on her shoulder, when I see the words in French on the worn letter below me: 'Please be the Godparents to our little Denise.' The letter was dated September 1972. I had just celebrated my first birthday with Papa's twin sisters who had visited us in our little house in Glenhaven, California. I only know that because there are pictures of this trip — I'm smiling, chubby arms and face, blowing out my one big candle on that three-layered chocolate cake. There's a picture of me, bow legged, taking my first step, reaching out for Papa's strong, tan, hairy arms. I don't remember him catching me but he must have. No father would leave his daughter standing all alone."

I tell my children about this letter. I wish I had it now so I could show them, but I think they understand, as much as they can at their age. Papa must have believed that my aunt and uncle would be the best ones to raise me if something happened to him and my mother. Godparents are more than a religious obligation in the Basque Country; they guarantee to act as surrogate parents if needed. He must have known that whatever disputes or differences they may have had in the past, as siblings do, that I would be safe and cared for at Irochbeheria, the home of his birth. I would eat well, learn to speak his native Basque tongue, maybe even learn to sew — something I wish I could do now instead of taking my buttonless shirts to the dry cleaners. I remember the emotion of trying to stop a tear that welled up in my eye, only to see that my aunt, who cries often and easily, openly wearing her emotions on her sleeve, was already there. Of course I can never know the depth of those tears and the complex thoughts and emotions from which they spring, but I did know then, as I know now, that she wanted me to know that I would always be welcome here, and I was never alone as long as Irochbeheria was standing.

I could feel the plane start to descend and the tears of joy and emotion welling up in my eyes as I spotted the first sight of the red-tiled roofs and white-stucco houses that line the Atlantic coast in Biarritz. The Basque coast (*kostalde*) acts as a bridge, a retreat, a market for the people of the valley. The ocean (*itsaso*) is like a provider that exists within the natural rhythms of life. The *kostalde* is a place where the arts of life, good will, and enjoyment all take place. Beyond the coastline are the white stucco houses with red tile roofs, nestled in rich farmland and throughout the rolling hills of the lowland Pyrenees.

Once inside the airport, we descend the stairs off the airplane runway. My cousin Peio, one of my nine first cousins, eight of whom all live in the same area in Lower Navarre, near Ortzaize — didn't show up at the airport as I had told my children he would. Although I was surprised, I didn't let it bother me. I have total trust in him after decades of shared experiences that no missed pickup at the airport terminal can erase. There is a bond that is both timeless and wordless. Instead, Beñat nudged me as I waited in line at Hertz in the Biarritz airport to rent our car for the three-week vacation. "Mom, there's Milen, waiting outside for us." "No, I told him empathetically, it can't be." (In my mind, I still see Milen as a newborn in a stroller in the center of the village square at the festival, with pink and white baby clothes and that lovely, perfect doll face with olive skin and curly baby hair). Sure enough, minutes later, the children are waving her in through the glass sliding doors of the airport and I, once again, as my children love to do, am proven wrong. Oh how time flies and does have wings. Here is my cousin Peio's daughter, a graceful woman now, not a girl, and certainly not that infant in the stroller driving to the airport to greet us. She's wearing a red blouse and beige trousers and a lovely white scarf that highlights her creamy tan skin and milky hazel eyes. Smiling from ear to ear, I can see she has dressed up from her summer shorts and t-shirts to greet us, realizing that this is an important moment for us to fly all the way from California to the Basque Country. I have so many memories of my family waiting for me at the airport, standing there, waving; stoic uncle, smiling cousins, teary-eyed aunt, all with their strong farm muscles ready to lift our luggage and whisk us away to the traditional aperitif of whisky or beer at the airport bar. This time would be different though, as we had lived here for two years from 2010 to 2012. I knew my way through the windy roads to our home village inland in the valley of Ortzaize and the surrounding villages in the low Basque Country that cover the valleys, woods, and forests, known as the *beterri*. The domain is known for agriculture, artisanal workers and their goods, and the Monday market.

Donibane Garazi

I followed my cousin's daughter in my rental car this time with the AAA online discount (I used to try and get the lowest fare I could) only to realize that I still had to pay the regular price at checkout. The veil of Basque mysticism had lifted a bit in the two years Chad, the children, and I had lived there, as memories of sacred letters of long ago were replaced with experiences like paying high prices for rental cars, mundane grocery shopping, and banking errands to Donibane Garazi (Saint-Jean-Pied-de-Port). In 2010, Chad and I sold all of our cars, rented out our house in California, left our jobs, taken the children out of school, placing them in French public schools where they didn't speak hardly any French, and left to start rebuilding the Mill House in the Basque Country. I remember clicking the submit button on my PC to buy our one-way nonrefundable tickets, knowing there was no going back. Chad did make great progress starting construction on the mill, the children learned French and made new friendships, and I got to know what it was like to live here. In the end, it was adventure, and although difficult at times, worth every minute. Yet, despite the two years of living here as a local, it had been three years since we left, and I could feel, thankfully, a bit of that mystery inside me again, that airy mix of anticipation and wonder, of distant memories recorded permanently in my soul.

    I drive away in my gutless French automatic car, not worth the extra euros they charged me, except for the amazing gas mileage, with Beñat in the passenger seat. I follow Milen, with Delaney, out of the airport parking lot and into the familiar route back home. As soon as we drop off our heavy luggage in our vacation rental in Ortzaize, we immediately drive into a nearby village, Donibane Garazi, to go grocery shopping. The culture shock hits me instantly as I realize I am searching for *jambon de Bayonne* (ham), *fromage de brebis* (aged sheep cheese), *confiture de cerise noir* (black cherry jam), and fresh baguettes at Intermarché instead of frozen pizzas at Safeway in California. Despite jet lag, I am energized, driving through lush green windy roads, smelling the misty mountain air reminiscent of past trips. I manage to prepare a meal for us at our *gite* (vacation rental), named Sabaia, in Ortzaize. Instantly, we head to our rooms, close *les fenêtres rouges* (red window shutters) and fall asleep. Although my dream is to someday rebuild the mill house Papa passed down to me, it is far from ready to live in.

 I wake a few hours later to my cousin Jeanine parked outside the bedroom window. I am happy that someone from the family has found me; being here means nothing without them. I motion her with my arms to come in as I lean from the window still in my nightgown. As is custom, we kiss on both cheeks and I offer her a glass of wine at the kitchen table. I immediately realize that I'm drinking wine having just woken up from a nap- "Oh, I'm definitely home," I think to myself as I smile inside. We talk about our trip here from California, the children, and our day so far. She's impressed that I was able to grocery shop and cook a meal, the house already stocked with food. I feel a moment of pride too, reflecting upon this newfound burst of energy. She tells me that the brother of the owner of the house just committed suicide this past week. He was found in the neighbor's pool. The dead man was also the first cousin of my uncle and godfather Jean Pierre, and knowing how close that family is I realize that this loss must be greatly impacting them as the internment (funeral mass) was just a few days ago.

 Later that evening, I tell my children about the death and explain to them that I have known many Basques who have committed suicide. They have many questions about this, as they should. All I can begin to explain is that they are a proud people, sometimes too proud, almost unbendable, and fiercely independent. They talk about success, not failure. And the older generation doesn't talk as openly and freely as we do. They have kept their emotions inside, perhaps as a way to protect themselves and their families from talk in the little village, as word travels fast and secrets are lost forever to rumor mills. Or it could be that as a people they have had to protect these secrets in the home to remain strong, to not be perceived by outsides as vulnerable or weak in any way. An invader could take advantage of this and the Basques have for centuries remained an intact culture in spite of no national border of their own in either France or Spain. I tell my children these are just my thoughts and I don't know exactly why someone takes their own life, but I do tell them that it is not the way to go. There is always a solution. There is always a way out of the darkness.

Despite the losses we endure, the years pass by and children grow into parents of their own, but the tenacious passing of time can't wipe away what brings me back to this little village time and time again. This is my spirit home, the place where I too will return someday when I cross the creek by Papa's mill. And Papa's mill house still stands. It waits for us in this little ancient village. It calls for us to keep living again. It speaks a story that is alive in us, a part of Papa alive in me.

Sunday, June 7, 2015

I wake to the distant sounds of roosters and the morning church bells as my alarm. To my surprise and amazement, we have arrived just in time for the *Fête-Dieu* (Corpus Christi), an ancient religious festival that has been taking place in this village and around the Basque Country for over 850 years. The costumes still resemble the design of Napoleon.

The Basque village and the rituals, traditions, and celebrations that take place in in it, are in constant relation with the perennial wisdoms of Nature and Mother Earth. Compassionate service and mutual reciprocity within the community are a shared experience of give and take. Life in the Basque village is a shared system of connections and relations where all beings converge and gather together. The villages are made up of quarters or *auzoak*, and the families established on the given territories. Traditionally, the man of the house, in each *auzo*, resides with his wife and family in one of the seven villages for the whole year. There are three networks within the *auzo*. Each network involves eight to ten households that share the same geographic area.

Fête-Dieu, Ortzaize

Neighbors are of paramount importance to the establishment of the *auzo*. A neighbor is admired and welcomed by other neighbors. Trades and exchanges of goods exist within the rule of justice and are based on the man's integral value. The neighbor unites with other neighbors. One cannot exist

Marching procession, Fête-Dieu

alone within the *auzo*. It is within mutual aid reciprocity and exchange of goods that relations are maintained.

The *Fête de Dieu* is a festival that brings together the entire village, neighbors and the *auzoak*, in celebration of God. I remember my first *Fête de Dieu* when I traveled here with Delaney, only fifteen months, to research for my dissertation on Basque Spiritualism. My cousin Annick had explained to me how this festival used to take place outside the church, in a lovely scenic spot overlooking the lowland Pyrenees Mountains of our village. Not having been raised in the Catholic Church but feeling so close to nature here, I could relate to this Festival of God, so primitive, simple and wholly.

Outdoor procession, Fête-Dieu

I had surprisingly planned very little for this trip. I had a list of seven items that I had hoped to check off. The *Fête de Dieu* was not on this list but I was thrilled that just by chance, I had awoken to the beating of the marching band outside my window. Visiting the Mill House, as the children and I planned to do, would have to wait for now. I took this detour in plans as a good sign, hopefully the first of many that God and the ancestors watching over us had in store. Above the crow of the roosters, the church bells tolling on the half hour and the band warming up down the cobble-stone street, all I could hear were the birds chirping, singing a song of remembrance. There are moments of silence here in between the sounds of the village that I don't experience back home in California. It's a silence that comforts me, holds and caresses me, like a baby in the arms of their loving parent. There is a safety here that I have longed for all my life. There is no more waiting for Papa to come home, no more longing for his return. There is simply living and being at one with this country that brings me back once again. I write quickly now, while the children still sleep and the day waits to be born. I feel excited in anticipation of what mysteries lie ahead in the next three weeks. I imagine the countless kisses on both cheeks, all the hellos and goodbyes and the long stares we will receive, as we are both strangers from America and Papa's children and grandchildren. After organizing flight schedules, reserving cars and "*gite*" vacation rentals, there is no more planning now, just waiting and wondering what will take place as I follow the procession of dancers, of flute and clarinet players, of young children dressed in white, throwing pink and red flower petals on the street as they march back and forth from the seventeenth-century church St. Julian to the open, lush green field outside. I will follow the procession, trying not to think too much about all the worries in my head, about trying to understand unspoken messages I may misinterpret here, and of life — the busy schedule and details of life that wait for me in America. Instead, during this Festival

> *There is a belief that the dead would appear in the form of light, shadows, or sounds. When this happens, you are to ask them what they want. Once their wish is fulfilled, they won't return.*

of God, I will trust and hope and believe that this one God is watching over us today and forever. And this family, this village, and this land is my home, and no one can ever tell me different. I know with a certainty that only comes with standing on this soil that I am both safe and free, like the bird that waits for me to open this window.

Early the next morning, after a heavy, peaceful sleep in my bedroom of refinished gray-and-white-stained furniture, mixed with finished-oak floors and thick-wooden high ceiling beams, I hear Delaney crying out for me down the hall. I leap out of bed, run down the hall, and enter her room. It is dark, except for the tiny ray of sunlight pushing its way through the closed shutters. The room is warm and the air is stuffy, so I instantly open the window just enough to let in some fresh air. The room needs to breathe and so do I. Delaney is sitting up in her bed, visibly shaken. "Mom, I had a dream about this old man at the ranch house (my maternal grandparents' old ranch in Lake County that is currently on the market to be sold). This old man came and sat down at the dining-room table and asked me if I knew the name Orpustan? He had gray hair, deep-set eyes, and a long, narrow nose. Then, I replied, 'Yes, I know Orpustan. That is my name.' Then, he looked at me sternly and straight at me, almost without emotion and told me to 'stand up for what you believe in.' Then, I woke up."

Right away, I knew that my father had come to her at the ranch, like he had come to me so many times before in my dreams. I knew this by the way she described this old man. I felt his presence as she spoke but I mostly knew it by how he introduced himself and what he told her. Delaney didn't know it was her grandfather, nor did I tell her; she seemed frightened enough. But that is how he had first come to me in my dreams when I was a young woman. He would ask me, ever so politely, if I knew the name Orpustan.

I didn't tell Delaney all I knew about ancestor visitations on that cool, crisp summer morning while sitting on the edge of her bed because I didn't want to overwhelm or possibly frighten her even more than she was. But I know how ancestor spirits present themselves, not just in the dreams of night, but how they manifest in the life dream of day. As my wise mentor Angeles herself used to say: "The Intuit people say: 'There is my plan, and then there is the Mystery's plan.'" Her dream was the Mystery's plan.

I decide that the best way to explain the meaning and purpose of this dream to Delaney is to share my own rite of passage into the Way of Wholeness. When I was twenty-two years old, lost, lonely, and afraid of just about everything, a Basque-American female cousin of mine, born and raised in San Francisco, was planning a trip back to Ortzaize for her summer vacation. I decided to follow. There was no reason not to go. I remember asking the "why not?" question and being unable to find an answer, I flew "toute seule," as they say in French, and like a warrior preparing for battle, I soared into the mass of gray-and-white clouds and didn't look back for two fun fête-filled months.

It was during that summer vacation that I not only developed close relationships with my aunts, uncle, and cousins in the Basque Country, but that I learned and understood where I came from. Although the house of Orpuztan is now owned by a maternal cousin of my fathers in a nearby village, simply seeing this house for the first time changed me. I was now part of lineage of generations of Orpustans who came from the house of Orpuztan, dating back, at least, to the 1200s. In front of Orpuztan is a small stone hut, most likely a shelter for pigs and other animals on the farm. When I look at the hut, I can cast a glimpse into a prehistoric past, an ancient time when my ancestors lived in small mountain caves.

Almost three years after that trip, at twenty-five, three seemingly random events forever altered the course of my life. First, I received a phone call. About 10:00 p.m. one normal middle-of-the-work-week evening, after the other roommates in the house I was renting a room from had gone upstairs to go to sleep, my unlisted phone rang. I was standing to the side of my phone, facing the north, staring at a blank wall, with a blank, empty heart.

Stone hut shelter (borda) for farm animals of Orpuztanea

A gentle, serene female voice calmly informed me, without asking who I was or what number she had reached, that they had finally found him. After twenty-five years (the same number of years my father had been missing), they (who was they?) had finally found him (who was he? my father?). Again, I froze. My body, my mind, and my heart stopped. Time stopped.

"Who?" I managed to utter, in this single, feeble attempt to speak.

"Oh, you're so and so..." she said. I stopped hearing at this point, so locked in my own fear that maybe, after twenty-five years, my father had been discovered. All my life I had been afraid that he had left us. Just now, at twenty-five years of age, I realized I had spent my whole life searching for a father that could, in all reality, have abandoned me.

The now cold, deadened voice on the other end replied, "Oh sorry, I must have the wrong number." Oh sorry, I thought to myself. What are you talking about? You can't just call me out of nowhere, say these things and expect me to believe that this was just an accident, some rare coincidence?

Someone called me, trying to deliver a message. I picked up the phone. It doesn't get much clearer than that.

I was driving home from work a week later. I stopped off at my favorite coffee shop. I changed from my dress suit into sweat pants and marched out into the end of February cool, crisp winter air. The lush evergreen hills above the Calistoga Valley reminded me of Ortzaize, but I could only see the hills, not feel their beauty. The rise of grapevines filled the air and circled the few clouds that hung over the misty valley floor. I tilted my tired head just enough to notice that the hills weren't singing to me as they once had. The emptiness in my heart could not be comforted even by their majestic beauty.

I turned left on a side street. I puzzled even myself sometimes. Why had I decided to take a walk here? I never did this. I always drove straight home, closed in by my redundant, busy thoughts, and worries, too caught up in my own head to notice anything or hear any calls that didn't sound familiar.

I looked up and slightly to the left, noticed that a round, stocky man with large black olive-shaped eyes matched my stare. I instantly knew he was Basque.

I asked if he was Basque, out of respect but I already knew the answer. He said nothing. I walked closer to the fence that divided us. After he studied my face and eyes for seconds that felt like hours, he told me his last name. This is the way Basques traditionally greet each other, either by their last name or the name of their house.

"Orpustan," I said. As quickly as the three-syllable last name I had so proudly spelled out for my American classmates and teachers in school rolled off my tongue, tears misted up in his eyes. "I looked for your father," he said slowly, as he gazed at the mountains that now stood closer to us than before. "Yes, I knew your father well."

This stranger now became like family. He stood facing me; his face shaded and checkered by the chain link fence that separated us. He proceeded to tell me things about my heart that only I had prayed about, prayed to a spirit that was now speaking with me. He told me, with the certainty of a prophet, that I had nothing to worry about. I would marry and he would be strong, hardworking, not lazy and dependent on me, but my equal. I would marry soon and all would be well with me.

From that moment on, every other word that flowed from his lips to my ears, deafened and muted in comparison to the pulsing fire and sweet taste of mystery and wonder that now filled my soul. As I walked away, my feet flying off the pavement and floating with the crisp leaves and the marshmallow clouds, a voice repeated to me — "from the hills, cometh my strength."

I thanked my father's spirit, as he watched me from above; perching his spirit restfully on the top of the mountain range that had suddenly become more beautiful than I ever dreamed possible.

A week or so later, within walking distance from the spot where I had met the Basque man, a bright orange '72 square back Volkswagen sedan caught my passing eye, parked at the intersection where I turn every day to go home from work. I quickly turned my car to stop and peek inside. The black vinyl seats and the torn cloth ceiling were just as I had remembered it. The smell of old exhaust coated the worn out charcoal gray carpet and I could still see my sister and I singing songs in the back seat as we drove to grandmother's house for Thanksgiving. I could see my mother holding tight to the wheel, holding on for life to the only memory she had of her beloved spouse — two darling young girls with deep, wide brown eyes like their father.

The Volkswagen sedan that my father left behind for us, that had become the vehicle that transported us to kindergarten open house, piano recitals, and into high school cheerleading practice, was parked, right here in front of me, after all these years. I knew it. Even though the paint had changed from a light blue to orange, there was no doubt that this was the car.

Still, I thought, there was no way this could possibly be. It had been years since my sister sold it to a friend, who then sold it to a friend, and so on. Curious, I called the number on the window. Sure enough, this man had bought it from a friend of a friend of my sister, in the same town where she had sold it. The car used to be light blue.

I received three signs; with the Basque man, the car, and the telephone call. Three weeks later, I met my husband, the love of my life. We were married two years later. My husband is hard-working, loyal, and kind, just as the messenger described.

I calmly explained to Delaney, as I sat next to her on her lovely queen size bed with the clear white netting, that she had nothing to be afraid of. She looked like a young princess with her golden hair flowing down her back and her wide blue eyes staring back at me, glistening with tears. I calmly but firmly tell her that this was a message and a gift. "Whoever the man was," I explained, "he sent you an important and powerful message." Delaney said that in the dream she had been thinking about how her volleyball coach last year had not been fair to her and wouldn't let her play even though she was a very skilled player. Delaney had stayed on the team despite this unfair treatment, even with others who had not been able to endure it and quit, she didn't back down. She didn't give up. I was very proud of her for standing up for what she believed in, mostly in believing in herself. I didn't tell her that it was Papa who had come to see her. I would let her find out for herself. She would need to learn these life lessons on her own. I suggested she write this dream down and start keeping a journal by her bed side. I thought to myself that it is no surprise she has the same types of dreams I have had. She is my daughter after all and Papa's granddaughter. It would only make sense that he would care about her in the same way he has fathered me all these years in the dark, when no one is watching, in the deep stillness of night, when the quiet village sleeps. He would come to her when she returned to his homeland, when she was closest to the home, land, and ancestors.

Lesson 1

Never give up on what you believe in. Believe in yourself as the self is tied to the family, home, village, earth, and universe. Stand up and believe in something larger than yourself. Nature is tenacious. Seed the question(s) of your life dream by asking for what you want and need, and by always having hope and courage. Pay attention to your sleeping dreams, write them down, for they will be the guiding light of your day.

2
The Way of the Ancestors

"A thousand generations of my ancestors have gone down into this ground. Sometimes when I walk through the aisles of stone, the smell of the ground rises up. It is old and familiar and I know instantly that this ground is in me ... I have been here in a hundred little graveyards."
— Robert Laxalt, *In a Hundred Graves*

I don't want to see my godparents for the first time at the festival. Out of respect and tradition, I must see my family first at their home. We enter the kitchen side door as I have always done. The kitchen door is a glass French door with a weathered, once white, lace curtain that gets opened and closed depending upon the rays of sun that beam from its southern direction. Even though my aunt has kept the front doors open since my father disappeared almost forty-two years ago now, I find it more comfortable to enter through the side door of the kitchen. It feels less formal. I feel like one of her daughters that way. In customary tradition, my uncle and godfather Jean Pierre sit down with us at the kitchen table and we share morning coffee and orange juice. Almost immediately, he tells me about the death of his cousin. He doesn't mention that it was suicide. Instead, he tells me "he stayed in his house too long." If someone in the Basque Country is depressed, they will say they are tired and will stay in bed all the time or never leave the house. Depression is not expressed in the same way it is in the United States and Western society. I empathize with their loss, as suicide is something I unfortunately understand. I feel for how tragic this loss is for the family and how deeply it is affecting all of them right now. All I can think to say is that "we must cherish those relationships that are important to us and hold on to them" but I'm not sure these words help. I can see the deep reflection and sadness in his face as he bows his head to look down at the kitchen table in silence. As we drink our coffee in the small white expresso cups, I look around the small kitchen with the blue-and-white tiles on the wall that still exist from the original kitchen, I flashback to my first visit with I was eight years old, dancing around the parlor with my cousin, pretending to play the guitar. Thirty-five speedy years later, my aunt, now almost eighty, is rocking her new great-granddaughter in her arms next to the pile of laundry ready to be ironed (she still irons her children and grandchildren's clothes to this day).

Women in Basque culture are viewed as strong and powerful. In fact, there is a folk belief held by many people about the power, or perhaps loving control, that many women seem to have in their family house. For centuries, women in the old country were given great responsibility in the Catholic Church, as they were once the priestesses and healers. There remains a strong sense of responsibility assumed by women in the rituals of the house and the funeral rituals. Perhaps one of their greatest responsibilities in ancient times was their central role in birth and death rituals. The woman, along with her first neighbor (*lehen auzo*), played a very important role in the death and bereavement rituals. Contemplation and silence the day after the death mark the time when bereavement begins. The dead are washed, clothed, and presented on the bed, which may be richly decorated. The room is rearranged (the mirrors covered), and doilies and candlesticks can be changed. Upon a chair with a special linen (*lonjera*) one places the cross that the first neighbor has gone to look for in the church. Upon the table one places a dish with the blessed water and branches of *rameaux* (laurel) to bless the dead during the visits. On the bedside table burns a candle next to a crucifix or a statue of the Virgin. The presence of this light is essential and we have seen different types of candles and lights, as well as their relative value and given circumstances.

Ancient tombstones in the graveyard, St. Julian church, Ortzaize

The first neighbor on the *hilbide* road on the way to the church is initially informed of the death. He is the one who informs the town hall and church. The *andere serora* (*serorak*), from the Latin *sorer*, is the mistress of ceremonies. She lives near the church and was sort of a nun. Upon hearing of the death, she hands the first neighbor the mortuary cross which he carries respectfully in the room. Then, she sounds the church bells to alert the village. The first neighbor, as well as the second, reunite with the family. The goal of the announcement (*hil abertitzia*) is to report the death and to specify the date of the funeral. The announcement is also made to certain animals (cows, sheep, bees, dogs) by the family. Finally, the announcement is made by the sound of the death toll from the church bells. This is done three times a day: *argitzian* (*egunsentian*, at dawn), *eguerdian* (at midday), and *ilhuntzian* (*iluntzean*, at dusk).

The carpenter in the village, along with the first neighbor, is charged with preparing for the funeral procession. The dead are dressed in their most beautiful suits or dresses and carried with their head on a cushion to the funeral. The coffin is presented in decorated fabric, of *verdure* (greenery). In Lower Navarre, the carpenter makes, against the entry door, a little chapel of fabric that he cuts and decorates with verdure, laurel, and a special fabric called "*hil mihisi*." The carpenter puts the coffin on two chairs and then places the candles in the candlestick given by the family or collected by the neighbors (each house writes their name on the base so they can get it back). A crucifix of marble bought by the first neighbor that will fasten on the funeral monument, as well as the *ezkoak* (candles) of the house, and waxes of bereavement, used at the church for masses offered to the dead, are two very important symbols used at this time.

As my uncle talks, I think about these ancient rituals and how the internment or funeral for my uncle's cousin must have included the entire village. Even today, the funerals are community events, as hundreds, sometimes thousands fill the village square and then the church. Similar to ancient times, there were three very important and consistent traditions in the funeral procession, which speak to a sort of domestic religion — the importance of the *andere serora* who may be like a mistress of ceremonies, the role and active presence of the first neighbor, and the placement of the people and in particular, the women in the ancient tradition of the candles (*ezkoak*).

St. Julian Church, sixteenth-century church, with a seven-sided tower, Ortzaize

The important role of the first neighbor and his spouse greet the visitors at the entrance of *eskaratz* (funeral meal). The hour that the funeral approaches, the neighbors dress the women in their heavy cloaks, aiding the men to fix their capes of bereavement and to tie their ties. The carpenter places the order in the funeral and distributes the candles and flowers.

Before the first neighbor opens the funeral, he holds in the hand the funeral cross of the church. The carpenter is followed by the clergy who precedes the dead, who is carried by his four first neighbors. The women, driven by the first neighbor, go to the office of argi zaina in Lower Navarre, the *ezko* of the first neighbors in a great circle.

The funeral procession then develops in a single file. The family follows the dead, men and women separated. In front march the first neighbors with the cross of the church, sometimes with torch bearers. Followed by the representatives of the church, the priest and the children of the choir follow the cantor who relays the songs/chants. The rest assist them and join the route and places at the tail, without any particular order. Everyone follows the hil bidia, the road from the house that reunites it to the church.

After our visit at Irochbeheria, we arrive at the festival, the center of the village in front of the church, St. Julian that has recently been renovated. The entire village center (*au bourg*) is freshly cemented and tiled. It looks both modernized and ancient. The village center is already flooded with people from the entire village and even tourists who come from afar to see this 850-year-old tradition. I spot cousins everywhere in the crowd and in the procession that is forming down the road. I stand with the children in front of the pelota court, also newly renovated, the same pelota court my father, as a young boy used to hit his pelota ball against to strengthen his hand and increase his speed. This is the pelota court that taught him to play as a grown man in San Francisco at the newly formed Basque Cultural Center, a game that is more like a religion, a constant staple of their cultural diet, as second nature as eating and sleeping.

I looked across the center of the village square and noticed Terexa sitting on the bench. I quickly rushed over to say hello, as I knew that I had to talk with her as soon as possible to schedule a day and time to visit the Institute of Cultural Basque in Uztaritze (Ustaritiz). I had visited this institute when I researched my dissertation, over fourteen years ago. She had walked me through the aisles of reference books and journals, helping me explore the elements of the ancient Basque world. I will never forget seeing the picture of the integrated ancient Basque world. I knew when I stared at that picture that I was remembering the deepest parts of my ancestors. I was seeing a new world that was very old to my soul. Now, fourteen years later, here I am, following these pathways all connected to this ancient world with the *etxe* at its center. We greeted each other with smiles and kisses on both cheeks. After the initial formalities had passed, I quickly launched into requesting to schedule a time to visit the institute where she has worked, collecting and compiling Basque research and literature for many years, probably twenty-five or more. As I asked this question, I could see the wheels in her head turning, those deep set dark brown eyes shining back at me, already in thought, already prepared to respond. With her rapid response, I knew that she was ready for me to ask this question. Like most of my encounters here, the word had already traveled about my research project. As my grandmother used to say, "the grapevine is very short." Not only was she prepared for the question, but she had even reflected upon the response. "Denise, would you like to come over for dinner and we can talk about your research some more?" "Yes, yes!" I excitedly jumped up and down inside myself, slightly embarrassed at how pushy and direct I must have seemed, forgetting how "research" happens here at a completely different and much slower pace. It is a research that is social in context, happens at dinner tables and over stoves in kitchens preparing dinner. It happens over aperitifs and long conversations that take their own unexpected twists and turns down an ancient cobblestone village road. We set a tentative date for dinner and kissed goodbye. The research had begun without any effort on my part. I simply showed up, following the path before me. This is how the entire three weeks would proceed, me just being here, fully present, with the intention of exploring this ancient Basque world. My presence would prove to be enough. The collective community of villagers would hold me. The land, home, and ancestors would protect me. The family would cherish and love me, and the research would find me in its own perfect way and time.

> *As Angeles Arrien taught in* **The Four-Fold Way,** *The Way of the Teacher is to "be open to outcome, not attached to it," to trust completely with nonattachment to the end result, paying attention and deeply listening, to the process.*

The ancestors are never forgotten for the Basques. Every step of the way I think about all that Angeles taught and modeled for me. Communications and lifelong connections with ancestor spirits are at the central heart and essence of Basque spiritualism. There is a strong sense of moral obligation for the living to give moral aid to the deceased as one of the necessary elements of salvation. Second, certain aspects of rituals serve as protections against the sinister properties of death. The fact that the living are somehow intercessors for the deceased is apparent throughout Basque funeral practices.

The Basques connection with their ancestors is directly tied to their relationship to the spirit and physical worlds (upper and underworld), the home, and the land. The communication with ancestor spirits is so directly tied to the house that it is sometimes thought that the house actually speaks to them (the inhabitants of the home). Thus, the title of this book, *The*

Mill House Speaks, reflects this ancient belief about the *etxe*; that is a living structure that is both sacred and the center of Basque life. These beliefs about the dead are manifested through particular death and dying rituals and practices, directly linked to the house. One believes that the dead will come back to visit the house and divide up the sorrows and go on living. Also, one gives them offerings of food thrown during the daylight. At the beginning of the century, dead children without baptism (or in the case where the person didn't behave properly, or conform to the normal Christians), were buried under the roof of the houses in each parcel of land called *andereen baratze* (literally "the women's vegetable garden"). The word (*baratz*) garden is tied to the *sépulture* (the site on the church floor that pertains to the household of the deceased), and to the names of the ancient stone graves and tombstones, known as the cromlech and dolmen (Gentilbaratz, Mairubaratz). The living communicate with ancestor spirits through making offering at the *baratz* or at the foot of the chimney. These spirits entertain or help families. They regulate diverse affairs left unfinished at the moment of death or torment the living who do not respect their objects that they have left, or who have not made the promises that they made to them. The footprints of the dead are left in numerous places in the house, if there is a purpose for them to be there.

Sometimes, the souls return in the form of honeybees. Offerings are placed before the family beehive. The bees are warned that a death has occurred, by the mistress of the house. Most often, the dead are perceived as the gust of wind (where the bodies strike up against the house), the lights, and the shadows. When they return to the house, they are not able to see anymore, not the same as they imagined it. They break the mirrors. It is a very important tradition that if the soul of a dead person appears, never turn one's back on them.

The dead always need the light and the food. In the evening, they return to the fire with the ashes (the dead need the light). The night of Christmas, they come in the house and track their prints in the ashes. The next day the family searches the fire to verify this. One scatters the ashes from the hearth to the direction of the four winds at the time of the death. The dead are united with the living. They are all placed together under the authority and protection of the house. In the fifteenth century, Gabriel Tetzel of Nuremberg noted that Basque women worshipped the dead by decorating valuable tombs of stone with plants and aromatic flowers outside the church and light candles in front of them. Due to this practice, they rarely entered the church.

The spirit world and ancestor spirits are an integrated part of the physical world. This integration takes place in both the underworld (sub-terrain) and the upper-world (sky). Divinities and ancestor spirits are believed to live in the underworld, while the heavens (stars, sun, moon, thunder, and lightning) is the upper world, believed to be a reflection of the activities that take place on the earth. Thus, to be a part of the spirit world is to live fully within the physical world, and to be a part of the physical world is to live fully within the spirit world. I learned how to live in this world from the modeling of Angeles. She taught me to —

Lesson 2

Trust in the process and be patient. Balance action with reflection. Work hard, but celebrate accomplishments, and take time for the dream of your life's work to evolve in the spaces between the activities of daily life. Nature is unyielding and strong, but unpredictable. Strengthen respectful connections to the past (ancestors) and current relations (family, friends, community), honoring both similarities and differences. Share your emerging life dream through storytelling.

3

The Way of the Home

Tuesday, June 9, 2015

I should have known that the research here would not take place in a library, but at the *etxe*'s kitchen table. I showed Terexa my printed out eighty-page manuscript I carried in my laptop bag all the way from California. For the first two hours, I shared with her my literature review and she gave me valuable feedback and supplemental readings to investigate. She shared with me some of her rare print books on Basque folklore and let me borrow a few that I would read on my trip. In between the spaces of exchanging literature sprung spontaneous emissions of short stories from my manuscript. When I spoke, she listened intently and intensely, the wheels in her mind turning, emotions in her heart churning.

    I asked her if there was any literature or collection of oral history stories of mystical experiences, of dreams that came true (clairvoyance) or mysterious events passed down through stories in the home that reflect the ancient spiritual beliefs. She directed me to her website of oral histories she has collected but none specific to the exact subject of clairvoyance. She did tell me a story, one that she had shared with me almost fifteen years ago when I came here to research my doctoral dissertation on Basque Spiritualism, the belief that the living communicate with the deceased within the home. I remember sitting at the table on the second floor library, filled with periodicals and books at the Institute of Cultural Basque in Uztaritze with her and my cousin Annick, listening in awe and wonder to this incredible story from the mountains.

"My American eyes can see, changing hues of green, oaks of lime and evergreen, and all the colors in-between. My Basque heart can only feel, a peace found by Papa's mill. Only there can I see a pasture of brighter green, immovable rocks, protecting golden streams. A family still sings. Endless in a dream of home."

"My great-grandmother, who lived in the hills above Ortzaize, lost her three sons in the war. She later lost her fourth and last son in a dispute in the village over politics. She had signs that things weren't right. She would see leaves falling on the ground all around her and objects darted at her, meaning restless spirits were in the house. The priest told her to write down a message on a piece of paper to her sons and leave it in the kitchen and wait. She waited, sat outside the window and saw the light flicker (light is a symbol for ancestor spirits). She then returned to the kitchen table. On the letter to her sons were the words written: 'You need a mass.' After the great-grandmother received the message, she lived in peace for the rest of her life on the mountain."

As Terexa told the story, I remembered how my uncle and Godfather Jean Pierre had told me this same story many years ago because Terexa's great-grandmother was also his aunt, and after the fourth son died, the mother of these four sons had no one to leave her house to she left it to my uncle's father. This house is the house where my uncle was born. I had thanked my uncle for sharing this important part of the story with me and when I did he turned to me with his sharp, bright blue eyes, more serious than I had ever seen him and said: "It was my father's spirit who tells the story; not me."

Prairie at the Mill House, Ortzaize

This story has many hidden meanings tied to the ancestors and the house. One, ancestor spirits are living and alive. They continue to guide the living through unexplainable and synchronistic events and through dreams. Second, certain types of death leave ancestor spirits caught between two worlds, the physical and spirit world, and when these spirits are caught in this way, they are believed to be restless spirits searching for peace for themselves and for the loved ones they left behind. The beliefs about the dead begin with ancient rituals and practices. To the Basques, ritual is order, and order is ritual. Strict compliance to traditionally defined ritual is not solely an expression of solidarity in the face of death but also a way of ensuring the deceased individual's orderly entrance to the realm of the dead. Failure to comply with ritual form may have some disturbing effects, such as souls that still wake up at night, implying they are caught between two worlds.

The conviction that the recently deceased pass through a transitional state before entering the next world relates to many customs throughout the Basque Country. In the past it was custom to open a window or remove a roof tile at the moment of death so the soul could leave. This custom has fallen into disuse, but many still believe that the soul may frequent the household or neighborhood before finally departing.

Those souls or spirits who are caught between these two worlds are referred to as intermediary souls. There are two types of instances where intermediary souls, or (*arima erratiak, arima errateak*), are present. The first instance is when there are incongruous events, or coincidences during the night. The second is when there are diverse warnings by nature herself, and more particularly, by the animals. Signs of bewitchment, curses thrown by a *belhagilear* (*belagile*, witch, sorcerer/ess) and other *konjuratzeak* are given to those who understand. In addition, these intermediary souls generally pertain to the young who have died, particularly in the context of defeat, force, and so on. The aged are treated differently in death. There is a natural preparation that accompanies their death and dying process. There is a sort of resignation of destiny, as if their adventure is already written. It is those unforeseen, more tragic deaths, where the intermediary souls have their purpose.

These intermediaries are always active, alive in the shadow, but are also known as the breath, deeply exhaled, or the activity in the anteroom behind the church. The dead do not disappear. Even the church does not dispute that these intermediary spirits exist, as they recognize them in a particular sense. For instance, from the dead infant, God will make an angel.

While the overriding emphasis in the various ritual activities initiated by the living is to benefit or assist the departed, it is also clear that the villagers believe that the dead can benefit the living. In the majority of *iru urrune* (*hiru urrun*, three masses) offerings (given in the village when there is a crisis or special intention), the purpose is mainly to convince the dead to do one's part. In this context, the dead refer to the souls that are in Heaven and are therefore in a position to serve as intermediaries between the living and the Deity.

There are stories that demonstrate the perceived relationship between the living and the dead, a relationship in which the latter depend upon the former for assistance. There are ghost stories in which a dead person appears to someone in the village. Stories of apparitions are less common now than earlier in the century, in part, no doubt, because the religious authorities actively oppose such beliefs.

The souls or spirits (*izpiritua*, *arima*) leave footprints. They aid in protecting the animals by getting them to the cowshed. This can leave a track that a fire will purify. These spirits accompany the emission of the last breath. It is in this view that one takes away bad luck by continuing to leave the windows open in the room where someone has died. The ultimate passage of death is a complex world, interconnected, between the spirit and physical worlds, the home, the ancestors, and the earth and sky.

The third meaning of this story is how it speaks to the interconnection and multiple relationships ancestor spirits have with the living. In ancient times, it was believed that the deceased would appear on certain occasions, manifesting in different ways, such as forms of lights, shadows, and sounds. When this happens, it is the belief that if the living need to ask the spirit what they want and fulfill this wish, as in the case of the woman on the mountain's letter written to her sons and the response to have a mass. It is further believed that when this wish is granted, the spirits will not come back again. Last, but certainly not least, the story speaks of the importance of the house, as a temple, a sacred place of worship and healing, that is connected to all of nature in the upper world and the underworld.

The house protects against outside influences as the site of rituals, prayers, and the passing on of stories. The rituals are bound to the hearth, which is the meeting place for the underworld. Prayers of worship are relegated to this sacred temple cave. One blesses the house with water and says: Blessed water conceived from heaven, bless this earth, that which leaves this house, and all bad things. To protect the house from fire, rising water, and to be delivered from hell, one recites prayers such as "Our Big Father," "Our Little Father," or "White." The fire also occupies a central position in the *etxe*.

There are various rituals that pertain to the central position of the fire and the hearth in the house. The fire is the sign of life and of property. A poker is thrown to dip into the water at night for purification. Ashes are placed by the hearth on the landmark of the property to establish ownership. The woman blesses the fire with a shovel by making the sign of a cross three times. On February 2, for the Chandeleur (Candlemas, this practice existed up until 1935), the father of the house takes a candle or *ezko*, the night before he goes to light it and offers the supper. He reunites the family in the kitchen. He lights the candle in beeswax. The family kneels down before it. Each member makes the sign of a cross, one after the other. The father places his in front of the first family member. He makes the sign of the cross with his right hand and holds the candle with his left. He then makes three times a revolution. The participant kisses the candle three times and the father then burns a lock of hair. Three drops of wax fall down to the right of the shoulder under the clothes. The hearth is also the central place of protection and affirms the existence of the house. To mark ownership of a house, one puts fragments of wood in the hearth to burn, when one acquires a new animals, they makes the turn of the fire three times. The fire and hearth is also the place where the men and women pray with the priest for the ghost of burials.

The hearth linteaux at Irochbeheria.

Linteaux (lintels) are found both above the chimney and outside above the front door. The decoration of the chimney and the objects that surround it attest to the importance the people give to the fire. In certain places, even the back of the chimney and the stove are richly decorated. Like the hearth, fire, and chimney, the house's entry door is sacred, as the riches of the linteaux decoration attest to. The linteaux are carved prayers usually above of the door of the house that designate the father and mother of the house, as well as the date of the construction and reconstruction. There may be two or three different dates inscribed differently on the same house. The engraved linteaux became more and more numerous by the end of the sixteenth century. They can become rich decorations or very simple. The most beautiful are often in Lower Navarre and in Navarre.

The linteaux is not strictly bound to the door. The linteaux vary by region and have significant differences. Generally, at the center one sites the outline of a cross. To each side of the cross one finds identical, symmetrical symbols, such as the rooster, the sun, and the lion. Diverse elements are arranged in a careful hierarchy. This is the same on the churches. The linteaux on the house signify the religious dimension and sacredness of the *etxe*.

The linteaux reflect the ancient spiritual belief of the relationship between ancestors, home, and nature. The linteaux are a symbolic representation of their ancient and sustaining cultural beliefs. Meaning is made out of everyday events and encounters in highly superstitious and also deeply intuitive ways that are in touch with the rhythms of the seasons and the rhythms of the human heart. Sitting next to me on the bench of the kitchen table, I could almost hear Terexa's heart beating and feel her mind turning. Turning directly to meet my eyes with hers, she asked, "Why are you doing this project?" Stunned and completely caught off guard by her directness, I froze for a brief second, trying to hide my shock. I have come to expect the unexpected here. Just when I think I understand the Basque ways of communication, I realize I know nothing at all. She reads my mind, picks up on my doubts and fears, and adds: "Are you doing this work for others, for your mentor, for this grant, for the Center, or for you?"

That's when it struck me like a bolt of lightning. I can still hear my mother's voice on the phone telling me she heard from someone at the Center that I was writing a children's book. Twice she had mentioned this and twice I had tried to explain to her that somehow she must have heard wrong. Somewhere in that very short grapevine that quickly travels from the Basque Country to the San Francisco Basque Cultural Center and somehow up to my mother in Lake County, she must have received the wrong message. I almost laughed inside myself, or perhaps it was a nervous laughter, some kind of release of the stress and burden of responsibility I had been carrying trying to create this perfect project in memory and honor of my late mentor. Without thinking, I blurt out to Terexa, "Neither." (Am I really saying this?) "Neither," I say it again, so I know it's really happening. "I'm doing it for my children. I'm doing it so they will know that wherever they go in the world-off to college, married, moving for a career — that the *etxe*, their Mill House, lives inside of them." I know that I want, no need, my children to know that the old ways, the lessons of the home, the ancestors, the village, and nature are passed down to them. And that they in turn will pass these wisdoms on from generations to generations after them — that the old ways still exist; that even death cannot break the spiritual and cultural Basque bond in America. I want them to learn the teachings I have learned about what is important in life and to know that these things, deep in their bones, with a certainty that is unbreakable and unbendable, unyielding and strong. When the thunder, lightning, and storms of life rip their worlds apart, they will come back to their Basque heart and find peace. This peace will allow them to be sensitive and compassionate to themselves and others, strong in their convictions and beliefs (stand up for what they believe in), and smart and wise in their decisions."

  Later that evening in my bedroom, thunder rolls outside and the wind pushes its way forcefully through my bedroom shutters. I feel the magic, the force of nature (*indarra*) in my soul, both comforting and exhilarating. The red candle flickers on my nightstand and I reflect upon what Terexa said to me after I told her what I really wanted to do, after I found the courage to tell her the truth. She asked me the questions I needed to answer. I now fully understand on every level the reason I brought my two children here with me on this trip, why I followed my heart back here to do this research, knowing on some deeper, felt, and unspoken dimension that the answers waited for me here, right under my nose, within me all along.

"You are the history; your story is the folklore," I heard her voice repeat as I dozed off to sleep.

I realize finally, that I am tomorrow's history and someday my children will remember my story, just as I remember Papa's. This story is unique. So much has been written about Basque mythology and legends but no one has told my story and Papa will never get a chance to tell his. I think about the Maya Angelou quote I have in the background on my computer at home: "There is no greater agony than bearing the untold story inside of you." Someday I will be gone from this world. I will be a gust of wind, a distant thunder that rolls across the Pyrenees Mountains. "My descendants will live on in me," as Miguel de Unamuno once wrote. And this small but important book will be a baton that is passed from one generation to the next. I'm just one flicker of light from an evening star in the vast universe of galaxies, but while I'm still here, I can be a light that shines as a guide to others, to help illuminate their life's path in the same way others have illuminated mine.

I reflect upon what Beñat said to me as we drove up the street to visit my close friend and my first neighbor yesterday afternoon. This family is very close to us as they also have a summer home in Clearlake, not far from where I grew up

*Walnut tree in the yard at Barberanborda,
the first neighbor of Irochbeheria*

and where I still live with my family. Not only have they been the first neighbor here in the Basque Country, but in a way, they have been the first neighbor in California. As our closest connection to Papa, they have always been the first family we communicate with when there is news with the Basque Country. We've also shared many BBQs and summer events at Clearlake, rode bikes as young children and shared stories from the old country. The first neighbor (*lehen auzo*) or "the first door" (lenbizikoati) have a very important role in the Basque village

> **The neighbor is family
> (Barridea aurridea).**

life as they have certain rights and duties of mutual aid and aiding in funeral rituals. The first neighbor is the first house on the road that one drives to the church. The first neighbor is first informed whenever there is a major event or crisis; birth, illness; death function of first neighbor to get the doctor, healer, or midwife. In case of death, first neighbor sends the members of their household to assume agricultural and household duties during the duration of wake until burial. The first neighbor even arranges for the funeral and sends for the priest and contacts relatives. The first neighbor lends tools or something that needs to be borrowed. The two households are even likely to enter into joint projects during the course of the year, such as sharing a common electrical or water supply system.

Before we reached our first neighbor's house, Beñat looks me straight in the eye and uncharacteristically says, "Your father would be proud of you. You're the only one that speaks to all of your family." I couldn't believe my twelve-year-old son was actually giving me a compliment! I turned to Delaney sitting in the back seat of the car to verify that I had heard correctly, "Did you hear that, your brother complimented me!" Perhaps the folklore and mysticism was already unfolding beneath my nose. Prior to my dinner with Terexa, I was too focused on my project to realize what was happening right before me. In the past few days, it had rained heavily forcing us to stay inside our vacation rental — no internet, no cell phones, no video games, no laptops to distract us. We had played cards, game after game of cards in the living room, for the first time ever! I taught Beñat solitaire, something I had wanted to do for years but until now had been too busy, or so I thought, to take the time to teach my son a card game my mother and grandparents had taken the time to teach me.

Yes, mother, this is a children's book, a book for the children, my children. It's hard to say it but Mom, you were right, and somehow, somewhere in the quiet pauses of conversation on the ever-so-short Basque grapevine you heard something I hadn't.

And Papa, what is your unfilled wish for us? Or, am I already fulfilling it for you, right here, right now, doing this work, being here with all your family, and not giving up on building our Mill House? Is that why in the last dream I had of you about six months ago, you looked at me sternly, almost angry, asking me, "Why do you keep looking for me?" I felt almost hurt and definitely shocked at your irritation.

Yet, after being here, sharing these stories in Terexa's home, playing cards inside with my children safe and warm from the electric thunder and relentless rainstorms, I realize that instead of me asking you what you needed to be at peace, you were trying to tell me that you are at peace when I'm at peace. Your wish is that my life dream is fulfilled, and the life dreams all those you loved and left behind when you disappeared in the hills above our home in Lake County while hunting on a cold, dark, snowy Christmas in 1972.

Friday, June 12, 2015

The sun finally peaked out enough today after three days of on and off lightning, thunder, and rainstorms. Restless and needing to get out of the house, we packed up the car for the afternoon and swam at the indoor heated pool in Donibane Lohizune (Saint-Jean-de-Luz). I'm always proud of myself for being able to navigate through the details of life here, like using the correct Euro coins and exact change for the dressing room and wearing the appropriate swimming attire (Beñat found out the hard way that they don't want children wearing their boxers under their swimming trunks), but we survived once more. I watched happy, healthy toddlers jump around the children's pool with their parents and grandparents while the kids slid down the water slide. Delaney and Beñat remembering the water slide to be twice as tall as it really is. When we lived here from 2010 to 2012 the children had taken school field trips here and as children do, they remember everything as being twice its actual size. I can still see the Northern California hills of my childhood in my mind as giant as Mount Everest when in reality they were no higher than bunny hills. I used to imagine Papa walking down the hill with his *makila* (walking stick used for herding) in hand, coming to our front door with the rabbit he had returned to hunt that dark night in December. There is an ancient Basque myth, still widely believed, that on windy and stormy nights a pack of dogs belonging to a mysterious hunter can be heard in the mountains. It is said that he was a man who obsessively loved hunting and who heard his dogs following a hare or rabbit when he was at mass (or saying it). This myth is similar to the mythical lord or man of the forest (*basajaun/baxajaun*), a spirit that is believed to live in the deepest part of the forest, in caves, or also as a guardian of a flock of sheep. This wild man of the forest has a hairy body, large beard, extraordinary strengths, and animal-like features. These forest spirits are seen as the deities of the woods. The opposite of these evil or devil spirits in rural folklore is Dionysus — the Goddess of Wine. I smile musing about how my name Denise comes from Dionysus, and I can't help wonder how similar this myth of the hunter is to Papa's story. I feel a deep still sadness when I think about how much Papa must have loved hunting to go back that night in search of the rabbit that got away.

  Later that evening, with the fresh mountain air and the stream of light from the setting sun set gently drying out swimming suits, the children picked cherries off the vine that the owner of the house, Jean Trounday, left on our patio table.

*Delaney and Beñat sorting cherries on the porch
of our vacation rental, Sabaia*

I took pictures of this moment because it was a sight I hadn't seen in many years, my children not only getting along, but enjoying a simple activity together outside in nature. The cherries are found in the wild here along with blackberry bushes that line the creek bed. It was a beautiful sight watching my children pick sweet, dark-red cherries one by one. The joy I felt was tinged a little by the thought of how rarely this happens at home. Our lives are so busy with school, sports, social events, and friends, and then when there is downtime it's a direct dash to technology — cell phones, video games, TV. In this technological world there is a disconnection with each other and nature. I had to come thousands of miles, across the breath of North America and the Atlantic to see this shift happen, to watch my children being children again, laughing and joking together (mostly by making fun of me but that's a sacrifice I'm willing to make). It's taken more bad selfies here and been videotaped dancing ridiculous moves just to entertain my techy California kids. To see them sharing this innocent and simple childhood moment on a peaceful summer evening after the rain thousands of miles from home was worth every bit of time and energy I had spent to get here.

Saturday, June 13, 2015

Jeanine calls the 1990 style flip up cell phone my uncle Jean Baptiste let me borrow for the vacation at seven in the morning. I had a list of seven places I wanted to see and things I wanted to do on my trip. Hiking Baigura Mountain in Ortzaize was on the top of that list since I had never done it before. I had made it halfway up when I lived here but I had suffered from chronic pain for ten years (scar tissue grew in my body like a garden after the C-sections of my both of children). Two laparoscopies and a hysterectomy later had left me in pain for ten years until three year previously I stopped eating wheat and gluten. This must have reduced the inflammation and in turn, greatly lessened the pain. I had even gotten a special steroid injection before this trip to ensure that I could hike this mountain. Nothing was going to stop me this time! The pain of all these years had made me stronger, both physically and mentally, but not without a price of course. Pain wears your mind down in the same way the snow and rain slowly erodes the rocks on this mountain. It chips away at your spirit and pulls you into dark places in your mind. I had learned a lot about myself during the ten years of this pain. It had taken me to doctors and therapists, but I wouldn't be healed, I told myself, until I hiked this magical mountain that followed me everywhere I walked in the village.

The mountains (*mendiak* or *goiherri/goierri*, highland) are the third domain of the Basque Country. Although the *kostalde* and *beterri* have ancient roots, the most ancient traces of the population and ecosystem come from the mountains. The livestock pasturelands; the streams and gullies; the ferns, herbs, and woods form an integrated habitat that climbs to high altitudes. There are sheep huts (*ardibordak* or *bordak*) on midslope mountain ranges where famers *bordazain*) and shepherds (*artzainak*) herd their flocks.

Ancient sheep hut (borda) on Mount Baigura

After all those years of wondering, Baigura was everything I had dreamed it would be. The vultures circled around the highest rock on the mountain peak, protecting their babies, then quickly whisked them away as we climbed closer to their home. I suppose Delaney and Beñat, if you're reading this now, you'll understand better why I never shared my depression with you. Like that mother vulture, I want you to have a childhood free of the worries I had growing up. I wanted you to have a strong mother who protects you, someone loves you unconditionally, would carry you away at the slightest risk of harm and stand by you through all times, times when you need a mother to listen and care and stand firm in her parenting. In the West, depression is still stigmatized as a weakness and I imagine the same exists here, but I can assure you this is not true in the slightest. Depression has made me the woman and mother I am today, the friend, the sister, the writer, the teacher. I can only describe my depression like falling off the cliff of Biagura and feeling like when you land, you can't get up, even though you want to, with all of your might, you can't move. Even worse, laying on the base of this mountain, stranded in the valley below, you see the train circling the mountain ridge coming your way but there's nothing you can do it stop it. This is how I felt when I fell into a rapid but severe depression eight years ago. I just couldn't stop the train from creeping down the tracks. But, it didn't kill me, like it has so many of our ancestors. I've heard suicide rates for the Basques are second only to the Japanese. I'm not sure it's so much that our depression rates are higher but because we haven't known how to get off the railroad tracks in time, or we've been too proud to try. I really think, in many ways, it's that simple. Because of my education and career background in social work I knew I needed help. I had to go to a doctor to get diagnosed because I thought I had the flu! I couldn't eat, couldn't sleep, and couldn't' function. Deep down I knew I needed help or I wouldn't get up in time to escape the train. Through the grace of God I found my way to an amazing doctor who slowly, over the course of a year, helped me see the sun again and run alongside the train instead of under it, but I am almost sure that without his help, I would not be hiking Biagura, watching you steadfastly march up this mystical mountain with me.

If you ever, ever find that you have fallen off the mountain or can't stop the train from coming, ask for help and know that you belong to an *etxe* and that the *etxe* is the foundation of the family and the village. The *etxe* connects you to your family, community, ancestors, and to all of nature in the spirit world. The house is more than physical structure with walls, floors, a roof, windows, and doors; it is the place for work, rest play, and worship. All parts of the *etxe* have double meaning-both physical and spiritual, as far as back as the prehistoric cave.

It is very important to understand that how the *etxe* is connected to all of nature through the upper-world and the underworld. The spirits of the sub-terrain world enter the house following a particular route; the preferred point for the meeting place is the kitchen with the fireplace, the mantel, and the opening of the natural cavities. The hearth is an outlet place for the underground world or a place of supernatural forces. It has a central and importance place in the kitchen and in the entire house.

The fire is a very important purifying element. A soil food presented to the fire is purified. The water collected at night is used for bad spirits by placing one red poker in the fire to ward against the bad omens. One also throws into the fire a grip of salt rock when the rooster signs at an unusual house or when one hears an owl. At the time of storms, one burns the blessed laurel (*rameau*) on the day before Easter.

The fire is also the sign of life, of property. It is customary to lay down ashes by the hearth on the landmark of the property. A circle of fire of an animal is made, as found in the expression *suhil* (fire dead). This signifies that the fire has gone. To count the families in the valley, one says, "there has been many fires."

The main spirits of the underworld consist of the following: Inguma or Galtxagorri, who comes and places itself in the throat of people disturbing their sleep. Sorgin, who reenters from the chimney to discover vials which contain magical substances. Maide, who borrows the same route to search for the offerings. Laminak, who come also in the night, exchanging gifts put down next to the fireplace, where they accomplish certain work. Mari: the celebrated Goddess lives also in the house, sited as the guardian angel who comes in the kitchen, as well as the Virgin.

The upper-world consists of the heavens in the sky (stars, sun, moon, thunder, lightning, diverse plants). The spirits of the upper-world are tied to the vegetation, mountains, as the earth shows that the sun is living. The sun and the moon, both circles, are reflections of the bright white of day and the darkness of night. Above the earth is the semicircle of the upper world; below the earth, the underworld. The wholeness of the two semicircles creates the whole circle of the earth and the heavens combined. The Sun and Moon are feminine divinities, daughters of Earth, to whose womb they return every day after their journey through the sky. The day belongs to the earth while the spirits and souls of the dead are believe do belong to the moon. *Urdina*, a Basque word, meaning the blue ring of life is the patterns that exist in life and death. The color blue of *urdina* reflects the relationship between the sky and the ocean. Alone, neither of them are blue, but together, in betwixt and between the sea and sky, shines the mystery of the never ending cycle of the blue light of life, death, and renewal.

The Sky

The blue sky is called Ostri. It encompasses the sinking stars and "scarlet seas" (*itxasgorrieta/itsasgorrieta*, place of the red sea) at sundown, returning to the subterranean world. The sky was believed to be the home place of the divinities. In the twelfth century, the word Urcia referred to God. The roots *urz*, *urtz*, *ortz*, and *pst* mean the light from the sky or the deified way they dedicated Thursday (Eguen) or "from celestial light" or "from the sun." Thus, Thursday reflected the supreme divinity of the sky and sun. The sky divinity (Urte, Orte, or Ost) was worshipped by the ancient Basques.

Lightning and Thunder

It is interesting to note that in Basque mythology the sun and moon are always feminine, as well as another revered celestial phenomenon: lightning. The twelfth-century divinity charged with the lightning, thunder, and flashes of lightning is Urtzi. This female divinity is charged with protecting the house from bad spirits by throwing a thunderbolt of stone or ax across the sky. She flows in a short cut to the sun.

The *etxe* is believed to protect against thunder. There is an ancient myth in which lightning is a special stone (Neolithic axe, knife, or point of flint) that sinks down to the seven levels of the earth. After seven years it slowly beings to rise one level per year until it reaches the earth's soil surface. From then on it protects the house against evil spirits. The minced stone, caught by a stone or knife, is launched into the sky, pushing the land, to a depth of seven stages. This belief corresponds to ancient rituals that relate to protecting the house from lightning by placing minced stone on the doorsteps of the house.

There is a custom of placing steel or stone axes, (bronze before steel was invented) believed to have supernatural powers, with the sharp edge facing upward during storm to protect households from lightning. This belief is evidenced by an axe from the bronze age found stuck in the floor facing up of the cave of Zabalaitz (in the mountains of Aizkorri).

The Sun

The sun (*iguzki, ekhi/eki*, today most typically *eguzki*), is revered above all else; she is considered blessed, sacred, and holy, even referred to as God's eye. Euzkadi, the name of the Basque Country in Basque, also means "people from the sun." The house is also related directly to the sun, as it is positioned toward the sunrise, oriented East-West. The linteaux, located above the house door, possesses a representation of the sun engraved or painted, as well as a number of sun symbols: circles, rosette flowers designs, roosters, and the lauburu (Basque cross).

The sun is a protector from evils. Each morning, the sun drives bad spirits, which had entered during the night, from the house. The sun is also believed to ward off evil spirits at night. There are legends of *lamiak* that lose their power over men when they are touched by rays of sun. The sun is in this way, integrated to the eye of God. In the morning, the Basques welcome the day and each other with "*egun*" meaning day and also the moon at its rising. A Basque evening prayer says: "Saint sun, blessed, so rejoin our Mother Earth." The sun crashes down into the sub-terrain world following the road of the Mother Earth, personified by the Goddess Mari. In some villages they greet the sun by saying *agur*, "goodbye," when the sun is in the west. In the region of Bergara (Vergara) they refer to sunsets and sundown as Grandmother Sun going home to her mother. In this regard, the sun is the daughter of the earth.

The sun is celebrated at the time of the summer solstice with fire burning rituals to ward off threats or enemies to the crops, such as wild beasts, toads, snakes, harmful pests). These rituals are intended to assist the magical forces that keep the sun on its yearly course. There are beliefs and rituals on Saint John's Day, such as taking baths in the morning to ward off sickness for the years, placing branches of hawthorn, ash, hypericin, flowers, ferns, and so on in the doors and windows and laying down herbs and floors at the front door to protect the house against lightning.

The Basque cross, the *lauburu* mentioned above, is actually an ancient sun sign. In addition, grave or funeral stones, linteaux, and front door decorations have sun sign symbols, in the form of circles, wheels with rectilinear and curved radii (*urbina* in Basque), pentagonal stars, swastikas, oviform signs and rosettes, the *lauburu* or tetraskelion in the stone of Santa Clara and found in the museum of Iruñea-Pamplona. The wild thistle placed over the front door is called *eguzkilore/ekilore* or sunflower, representing the star. The wild thistle is believed to ward off evil spirits, witches, disease, storm, and lightning.

The Moon

The moon (*ilargi*), is equally revered and is of feminine gender. She is called Grandmother Moon and mother and "the mother of the moon is the earth." The moon is sacred. Children are taught that the moon is the face of God and they pray to see her rise. The moon is greeted as "Holy Grandmother Moon, may God bless you; may my astonished eyes bring no harm to you; may all who see you speak to you in the same way."

In the home, one finds a half moon engraved on the linteaux and the furniture. For instance, when the moon is waning, one should cut trees whose wood should be used for making furniture and tools. Much human activity is relegated to the cycles of the moon (the calendar). The moon is thought to have beneficial influences on plants and animals. There are beliefs about cutting down trees and the gender of people or animals conceived, depending upon if the moon is waxing or waning.

The days and nights are clearly very different times, marked by the presence of the sun and moon. It is the expression: "the day belongs to the man of the day, the night to the man of the night." Saint John and Saint Joseph come in the night to the bed. Another saying devoted to the day and night is: "today give me a good night, after this night give me happy dawn. God, you give a good night." The days of Friday, Sunday, and Monday all have root words that correspond with the moon.

Ilargi for moon also means light of the dead (from *il*, "dead," and *argi*, "light"). It is believed that the moon illumines the souls of the deceased. It is also possible that the names iretargi and *idetargi* are related to the names of the night spirits of Ireltxu, Iritxu, Iruztargi, and Idittu, according to legends from Bizkaia. There are also spirits of the dark night, such as Mahuma (also known as Mamurro or Mamurra). Mahuma's activities are relegated to difficulties in the night, such as nightmares oppressed by the heart and difficulties breathing during sleep. The scarecrow, phantom, monster, and insect are also related to spirits of the night.

The Stars and Stone Circles

As early as 4000 BC people were looking up, making shapes out of the stars and using those constellations to retell their stories. Rosyln Frank has discovered more than twenty-five years ago mysterious, almost perfect circles on rocky slopes and plunging mountainsides of the Basque homeland. Mapped by a center stone and eight outlying stones-four marking the inter-cardinal points on the perimeter of the figure-these stone octagons have been built by the Basques for thousands of years.

The measurements used in creating the stone octagons only confirm Frank's understanding of a culture's ability to bring the stars down to earth and put them to practical use. The stones are positioned to the north, south, east, and west. Frank has reasons to believe that these octagons actually reflect a coordinate system, a ritual manifestation of the system used in mapping and navigation, with the center stone representing the North Star." These octagons are an unusual shape and size and a diameter spans nearly a thousand feet, laid out across some of the roughest terrain in the mountains. They established legal and social boundaries and the Basque shepherds still used these stone octagons to map territory they would use for winter and summer grazing.

In the Middle Ages, hundreds of years before the invention of the decimal metric system, the Basques measured things in units called *gizabeteak* (based on human size and/or height) and performed mathematical calculations using multiples of seven. Only the Basques retained the septarian value for the league, a value that fits precisely with the earlier coordinate system used in navigation and mapping. Clearly, the ancient Basques were connected to the earth and sky with an uncommon understanding.

Stars and Bears

The Basque version of the legend tells of Little Bear (Hartzkume), born of a human woman and a mythical Great Bear, who is teased as a child because he's very different. Across Europe and to the northeast, bear stories are remarkably consistent, remaining almost identical in areas hundred miles apart. The constellations of the Great Bear and Little Bear rotating around the North Star were used to tell stories and perform rituals related to the bear. Some of the helper animals found in the folktales in the Basque Country also appear to show up in the sky above-the Grey Mare killing the Black Wolf (Centaurus and Lupus) along with the Female Eagle (Aquila flying along the milky way).

Over the centuries bands of performers, called jesters, reinforced the common belief that bears held special powers, that humans descended from bears, and that animals and humans lived together in a symbiotic relationship to earth. Such ideas were most certainly pagan, a threat to all those

Inquisitors who demanded loyalty to one god and one church. The adventures of the Bear Son, Hartzkume (linked symbolically with Ursa Major and Ursa Minor), remain today in the stories and rituals performed in the Basque Country. Variants of these stories and similar rituals are connected to these earlier beliefs that humans descended from bears, in which Bear Son, half-human and half bear, act as an intermediary between humans and their bear ancestors.

These stories indicate a strong resemblance to those of shamans and are not unlike those of the Native American vision quest with its animal helpers and medicine bundle. In the archetypal tales of the Basque Country the shaman apprentice is accompanied by Spirit Animals Guardians who also play a major role. Such helper animals are a common element in shamanic cultures as in the vision quest.

Like the intertwined symbol of the Lauburu cross, the Ancient Basque World is integrated, alive, dynamic, and meaningful. The ancient rituals, practice, and stories provide spiritual roadmaps that guide moral conduct and peaceful collaboration for the individual, the family, the home, and community. As one carries out daily tasks and activities in the house with family, one is building character. In this way, the *etxe* is the place of truth and honesty. One cannot deny their truest nature within the house. As one is honest with who they are and what they need, then goals, visions and life dreams will be nourished and protected. Although character development continues in all areas of life, the central, core place for building character takes place within the home.

The Way of the Home is the Way of the Visionary. All of nature is connected. Knowing one is never alone and always tied to the house, one has the capacity to see the light when there is darkness, to find a way out of the winding caverns and into the light of day, to sing when others lose their voice. Yet, paradoxically, it is only through struggle and pain that we can come to know the purity and fullness of joy, of absolute inner beauty of self and to exude toward others.

Being truthful means fulfilling one's word. Keeping oral promises is extremely important in the Basque home and village, as it demonstrates trust and respect, the foundation of a safe and healthy community. Having respect for others means respecting their word, actions, and deeds.

When we speak our truth without blame or judgment, and see what is possible in others, we begin to see their light and understand their moons, or darker side. Then our visionary illuminates and guides us further toward fulfilling our life dream and purpose.

Like the house, whose more than just a material structure, whose roles are to assimilate, produce, grow, interact, and reproduce, the individual exists within a larger network of relations within and outside the walls of the house. The house is definitely in firm relationship with the entities of the sun, moon, thunder, and all the elements of the earth and Basque life. To live within the context of the *etxe*, is to live in connection with the values and bonds of the community.

The Visionary can see this when others cannot. As Angeles once wrote about the Visionary in **The Four-Fold Way***: "Tell the Truth Without Blame or Judgment." When we express the inner Visionary, we know and communicate our creative purpose and life dream, act from our authentic self, are truthful, and honor the four ways of seeing.*

Lesson 3

You're never alone. Nature is all around you, interconnected and interdependent. Nurture yourself and others, discovering all sides to your place in this world. Be honest and tell the truth. Be true to yourself and others about who you are and what you need to nourish and grow your life dreams. Incubate your dreams with gatherings in the home—meals, song, celebrations, and birth and death rituals.

4
The Way of the Land

"You have a gift; don't abandon it."
— Robert Laxalt, written a letter to the author, 1993.

The peaceful feeling of hiking Baigura stayed with me all through the night into the next morning. The wild horses watching us slowly make our way past their grazing on the mountainside, the mist covering the valley of Ortzaize and Arrosa (Saint Martin-d'Arrossa) below, their red rooftops getting more distant and smaller with each step we took, the deep green moss forests as we entered and exited the mountain with the ancient stone hut hidden in the dark corners of the valley.

There is an old Basque legend of a little bird that always tells the truth.

The pride and joy I felt watching you two courageously hike this mountain for three hours without complaint, without question as to why I must do it. Perhaps you do understand more than I think you do about what this journey means to me. I love you both more than life itself. I would hike the tallest mountain peak and endure the worst pain to save you. I would pick you up and carry you away from danger, and fly you to another nest if that meant losing my life, I would. You are never alone.

Sunday, June 14, 2015

I peacefully wake up this morning with the rising sun. The sky is a bright blue with only scattered white clouds dancing over the brilliant green pastures below. Despite the perfect beauty of this place, my mind begins to wander, worrying that I don't have enough information to write this research project. Then, I remember what Angeles used to say to me about the mystery's plan and how it follows its own pathway. I then think of all the quality time I have been spending with the children — no technology, just cards, hikes in nature, dancing crazily in the house, and telling stories of my family and this place; stories they will keep forever and someday pass down to their own children. Yesterday, when we finished our hike of Baigura, Beñat asked me how our mill and land will be divided after I'm gone (he had overhead me talking about how my father inherited the little house, the mill, and the land from his own father before his father died). I told him exactly what my aunt and uncle had told me many years ago when I first glanced upon this magical land. "The land and mill shall never be sold but always kept in the family. You and Delaney can share it if you choose. When the mill is restored as a house you can take turns vacationing here with your own family, and when they are grown, it will pass on to their children and their children for generations to come." I thought about how I need to get a special trust in place so that the mill can never be sold. I wish my father would have written his wishes down on paper, but at thirty-one years of age, he apparently had no plans of leaving this earth so young, and certainly no plans of leaving his mill house behind before restoring it. My mom told me that he had hoped to return someday, as many Basque immigrants had planned to return and run a trout farm. People in American often ask me why Papa left his village. I tell them that he had no place there anymore. He didn't inherit the *baserri*, it was passed to his oldest sister and her husband. He wasn't an academic intellect like my uncle, Jean Baptiste, although from all the stories from family and friends that I've heard over the years, he most certainly could have been. I understand my father was very intelligent but he preferred wild nature to the classroom. He couldn't stand to be inside too long. And, as a young man, he had most likely heard stories about the riches to be found in the great Wild West. Curious, bright, full of energy, and a romantic, he followed in the footsteps of his friends and neighbors, packed his *makila*, his English-French dictionary, enough clothes for a few days, and bought his ticket to San Francisco to arrive in a boardinghouse owned by Basque immigrants who would see him off to the Sierra Nevada where he would spend two years completely alone with his dog herding sheep in a hut on a mountaintop. America made men out of many young Basque boys.

 I look at my reflection in my bedroom mirror, wondering how much I am like my father. I wonder how much of my children are like him. Beñat is sensitive, smart, and strong-willed, character traits of many of my Orpustan ancestors and Delaney is intuitive, independent, and also strong willed. I long to know more stories about Papa growing up here in this village. What was he like as a young boy, a teenager, a young man? Yet, when I gently open up conversations about Papa with my uncle and aunts, there is nothing but silence. One afternoon, I walk up the winding cobblestone road to Irochebeheria to visit my family. When they ask me about my work sitting outside on the picnic table, I tell my uncle and cousin that I would like to hear stories about Papa in his youth. I am well aware that this is far too direct of an approach then they are comfortable or familiar with as their tradition and custom is to take long hours over aperitifs and long meals of barbequed baby lamb to share private and meaningful stories of the past. But I don't have much time. I have three weeks here, three weeks to gather enough information to write this project. I force my way into my aunt and uncle's kitchen with Delaney. We sit at her kitchen table but still no stories.

Leaving her kitchen, I realized what I had known since I first visited Irochbeheria the morning before the Fête de Dieu. I had felt an uncomfortable distance and now I would knew why. It was very important that I, the daughter of Papa, stay here on my vacation. Communication about such important matters needs to clear and direct.

It is important to understand the meaning of us staying there. Not only does the eldest son or daughter inherit the *baserri*, the house is always open to the siblings who are born in the house. Further, the matriarch of the house is often responsible for caring for family members in the house. When Papa died, my mother, sister, and I would always stay here. Not only was there a sense of responsibility to care for Papa's family but my aunt has left the front door on her house, the house of Papa's birth, unlocked since he disappeared December 23, 1972; that is almost forty-two years ago. Even though the chance of Papa waking through the French doors is almost impossible after all this time has passed, she still leaves the doors open if he ever returns. She holds on tightly to her beliefs, as do many Basques. When someone dies in the house, they close the window with cement and never open it again. When a young man disappears in America, they send him a message and his family a message that he is always welcome back home. This message has extended to his children and his children after. For the Basques, when a child is born in the house, he always has a room to sleep and food to eat if he is ever to come back home. Above the fireplace mantel, the linteaux reads in Basque: "All who enter here are welcome."

Because I'm as stubborn as many Basques, I too am slow to admit when I have made a mistake. When I return to our vacation rental that evening I pray to the ancestors for guidance from above and peace with my family, but mostly I pray to Papa. If Papa had lived, I think to myself, I would have better known the old ways, the subtle but profound family and ancient cultural traditions of my family. "Papa, I am here. I am listening. If you have a story to share, I would welcome it. Beñat and Delaney wait for the *etxe* to speak."

And speak it does and listen I do.

I wake up the next morning as the birds are chirping the sweetest song outside my bedroom window. The children sleep and the village is quiet. My mind and body feel heavy today, tired from the difficult clash between old ways and new, between ancient tradition and the modern world, between the bird who stays perched outside my windowsill but never travels far, and the bird who has been set free. Above all, in my heart, I know that this has been yet another test of the power of unconditional love, a love between family over little things that have big meaning, buried, with layers, untold, hidden stories that I am certain I haven't heard yet.

I cried yesterday when I walked away from the visit, a deep and long belly cry. It wasn't the first time I had broken a Basque code of conduct. I once sat on the wrong bench in church, not knowing that certain areas are tied to family homes in the village. I regretted that my daughter saw me this way but after some thought I realized that we all need to cry sometimes, even Basques. When I'm sad, I cry. When I'm angry, I talk. When I don't understand, I ask. I make mistakes. I read wrong cues. I'm completely and totally human. And despite my stubborn pride, I too know that I am not always right, although I am very slow to admit it, something I share with thousands of generations of Basques that came before me, and will surely come after me when I have passed.

Life changes people, and after years and years of wear and tear, of loss and disappointment, of regrets buried beneath the surface, a bitter wall can build, so that it can no longer hear the sweet voices of spirit, of distant chirping birdsong. I remembered Terexa asking me why I am doing this project and my realization in the core of my being that this project was for my children. That I want them to carry in their hearts the best parts of their ancestral culture; I want them to feel the united connection with nature I feel so strongly here, so that one day when I have passed, they too will feel a gentle breeze upon their back and know that I am here with them. I want them to know that when life throws them in the whirlwind of unexpected crossroads, when there are many choices to make at once, that they find the courage to take the pathway that is unique only to them. Every life is special. No two human beings have the same fingerprint. Each being places their imprint on the world like no one before or after them. I want my children to sing out loud, to dance when they want to dance, and celebrate after working hard and feeling proud of their accomplishments, knowing that the best comes to those who don't give up. When life gets hard, don't give up on what matters most, and stand up for what they believe in even when you feel alone. Beñat would often joke with me at home when we were playing basketball and I would make a very rare miraculous three-point shot, or when I was playing cards and guessed the color and number; he would poke fun at me that it was Basque Mysticism, as he knew that for years, I had been studying, writing, and researching it with the guidance of my mentor Angeles. But what he didn't know until this trip is that I had been living it.

He would often ask me what is Basque Mysticism and I always struggled to answer in concrete ways, in a few simple words. As I write now in this *etxe*, I see Angeles standing before me, I hear her voice, and see her words in my writing. I remember our last meeting together on January 23, 2013. My husband, Chad, and I had driven the three hours from our home in Lake County to Sausalito to meet with her. We had not met face-to-face since I had returned in 2012 from living in the Basque Country for two years.

Taking a day off from work and daily responsibilities was never a question when it came to meeting with Angeles. She always took priority because I knew, on some very deep and cellular level, that what we shared with our interest in Basque Mysticism was special, something otherworldly, something of higher purpose and meaning.

When we arrived, she greeted me in her Sausalito office meeting room, spacious and light, always with a fresh bouquet of flowers centerpiece on her long table. "You look more Basque now," she darted me with certainly that springs from thousands of years of ancestors speaking in quiet voices inside her soul. I knew she didn't just mean the dark brown hair, the long narrow nose, or the deep-set chestnut eyes. She meant the essence of my being was now more Basque — more centered and grounded, more self-assured, more focused and directed, stronger, wiser, clearer about priorities, purpose, and what matters most in life and in death.

Our meetings never lasted longer than twenty or twenty-one minutes to be exact. Whether they were phone calls or face to face meetings, they were short, brief and to the point, yet never lacked complete spontaneity, fluidity, joy, and heart. We shared stories and talked about all the societal changes taking place in the Basque Country today, from cell phones to American fashion and music, to shifts in thinking from old ways to new. We talked about what hadn't changed- the older generation who still remember days when letters came after weeks of waiting, when *amatxiak* (grandmothers) retreated to their bedrooms in reverent silence when son's went missing, or in happier times, when returned visits home to the Basque Country meant days of feasts and festivals, honoring immigrant shepherds, bakers, butchers, and restaurant owners for daring to leave the small village of their birth with nothing more than dictionaries, makilas, and the clothes on their back. Those were the days of the American Dream and the pot of gold waiting at the end of the rainbow, met with the reality of long, stark, dark nights alone for years in the Sierra Nevada or the Idaho mountains herding sheep, singing songs and chants from their youth, longing for the safety and comfort of a familiar world so unfamiliar now.

She mentioned again how excellent my article was integrating the three portals of the home, land, and the ancestors, three elements of Basque culture, universal to all collectivist, indigenous groups. She was always generous with her compliments and genuinely so which made it so much more gratifying to hear. Our faces would shift from smiles to somber seriousness, as topics swiftly shifted, like the wind, as there was so much to cover, yet the essential purpose was always the same — to continue our shared interest in exploring and understanding the elements of Basque Mysticism, and their application to help others, both in the Basque Country and in the West.

She leaned in her chair, posture upright, hands folded on the table before us. Bowing her head, fixing her eyes on mine, she said, "I have a project for us." I tried, as always, to remain calm and listening, without exploding in enthusiasm or falling off my chair. We had talked several times since our very first meeting thirteen years' prior about collaborating together on a project, but over the years, I had realized that our collaboration was already taking place. With each conversation with her I had come home to find a soul and spirit so close to my own. I hadn't always realized how similar we were, although looking back now I can see that, of course, she had.

We would "collaborate on a project to translate the legends, myths, proverbs, stories (folklore) from around the world on Basque Mysticism prior to Catholicism in one central collection." We would research the writings of those elder Basque Mystics who converted to Catholicism as Jesuits Priests but who, in their conversion, still held some of the old ways and beliefs, integrated within their religion.

The Basques were one of the last people in Europe to convert to Christianity in from the sixth to the tenth and eleventh centuries. Many of the ancient myths and beliefs of the Ancient Basque World, including their religion and traditions, disappeared with the introduction of Christianity. One such legend comes from Ataun, Gipuzkoa. It is believed that the villagers noticed aluminous clouds moving toward them from the east. The villagers, frightened, sought the advice of a wise elder who told them: The Kixmi is born and the end of our race has come." Kixmi meant monkey, the name the ancient Basques used to refer to Christ. Following the miraculous cloud, they all came toward the valley of Arraztaran where they hid under a huge gravestone or jentillari in Basque. According to the legend, the ancient Basque religion came to an end.

"You will be more famous than Joseph Campbell," she beamed at me. Did I want to be more famous than Joseph Campbell or did I just want to work with her? Still, without hesitation, I just smiled back and nodded and followed her lead. I trusted that she would guide me in her wisdom to translate the messages and lessons from the earliest Basque literature, messages that are primarily codes of conduct and integrated into a nature based belief center. I knew, without a doubt, that the three main portals to understanding the ancient Basque belief system and mystical ways were through the home, the land or earth, and the ancestors. Basque Mysticism is deeply embedded with the natural world, integrated, whole and united.

The ancient Basques were primarily an oral culture, where spiritual traditions were passed down from generation to generation through legends, myths, proverbs, and stories. These stories provide clues or coded messages to their mystical beliefs. Oral storytelling, *bertsolaritza* (a spontaneous singing duel of poetry and song) music, song, ballads, stone engravings on tombstones, and linteaux above the house entry have been how the Basques transmitted these ancient spiritual beliefs, moral codes, and life lessons. Another mode of transmission includes birth and death rituals, celebratory festivals, and dances such as the *zamalzain*, the oldest Basque folk dance and once of the most ancient in Europe. This ancient dance is really a pagan fertility dance that celebrates the coming of spring. It is a dance of good against evil, beauty against ugliness, and a man's eternal battle to conquer his circumstances.

She was going to work on getting a grant to pay for my time and the translation services. She said she was going to write me into the grant this summer so we could start our work in the fall. We talked about how busy I was and how I would need to free up some time to do this. I told her that this project was a top priority.

Then, I realized why she had broached the subject of my busy schedule. She was trying to feel out if I could be the one, if I could be the messenger to carry the message from generation to generation, from ancient Basque World and mountain caves, to modern times of busy highways in an internet world.

"Denise, I'm on the short side of the hill now, coming toward the final years of my life." "I need someone who can carry on my work."

Before, she could go on, I started to tear up. Then, completely unlike her, so did she. There was silence, that silence we know from sitting on top of the highest peak in the Pyrenees Mountains, when the wind swirls around you, and vultures circle above your head, when the clouds separate and all you see is bright, bright blue against evergreen slopes and lush vineyards. A silence that is found at the dinner table when an elder speaks about life lessons that comes only from loss and the profound sense of love that follows and endures across oceans and continents. The silence that resonates in our soul, a peaceful joy and unshakable knowing that the Basque Spirit is the spirit of all people, the truths we know from our ancestors are the truths so desperately needed in our ever-changing America.

"Of course, I will." "I had always felt it, known it but to hear you say it is . . ."

"Thank you. Thank you," she uttered beneath her breath, and that was that.

The rest of our meeting was passing time, just being together and sharing our worlds. She walked me outside, like a mother to a daughter, and waved goodbye for the last time. Although I didn't know it then, I would never see her in this life again.

I had promised her that I would carry on her work and our interest in Basque Mysticism, and in the Basque tradition, giving your word means everything. I just didn't know then that what we were searching for was within us all along.

The Warrior within shows up and chooses to be present. There is no other way to manifest your Dream than to show up and be present, as Life's Mystery unfolds. As warriors, the Basques showed up to defend their land and homes against countless invasions, preserving their language and cultural tradition without national borders. The Basques still today protect their village constantly looking out for each other, by being involved in a circular process of give and take, of sharing goods and services. This process of mutual reciprocity requires the visionary to see what is possible in others, to honor one's word, to respect others and be willing and able to give and receive. This give and take of mutual reciprocity is how Basque farmers are able to successfully maintain their ancient artisanal and organic agricultural practices in the village. Mutual reciprocity is a core value and generosity is a character attribute that has preserved the ancient Basque culture. Patterns of interaction include exchanging food and goods, but even go beyond that. Two or more households in a network may rent a truck together, bring in straw or purchased hay, rent a vacant farm to use jointly in the winter for sheep pasturage or animal husbandry, or agree to share wood fire for the winter and cooperate in transporting wood to appropriate dwellings.

The members of the *auzo* have formal visits to one another in specific circumstances, called *vizita*. The specific circumstances include when a baby is born — all the ladies in the *vizita* network have an obligation of attending an "infant lunch." The women are invited to the newborn's household. The baby is brought out for everyone and in turn the visitors have a gift offering chicken, wine, or money. When there is illness visitors give refreshments and leave a gift. When there is a death the women attend the wake and vigil of the corpse, discuss the details of death and plans for the funeral.

I remember everything that she taught me but most of all, I will never forget the day I heard of Angeles's passing.

I danced that morning for the first time that I can remember in a very, very long while. I danced free style in my living room, peering up through the open skylights, to an expansive spring sky. I can't tell you why I danced that morning except that I felt a part of my spirit open up to a free and heightened joy I hadn't felt in some time.

    Later that afternoon, I drove out to visit my therapist. I had just started therapy a couple months previously to try and slow down and enjoy my life more. I lay down on the couch, and closed my eyes. It was then that I was someplace else; someplace between earth and sky, between this world and the other. I closed my eyes and held back the tears of emotions welling up inside me. I missed my cousins in the Basque Country. I talked about the closeness we share, the deep connection to place and family that is both of this world and completely part of another. Then, I felt the chills and deep dark sadness in every cell and bone in my body. "Oh, how beautiful she was — how hard it was to lose her; how much she is missed by those who loved her most." Was I talking about my aunt in the Basque who took her own life? I thought it was my aunt I grieved but then something shifted in the space around me. I could see in the black expansive night sky with the distant blue stars around, a bolt of flames dart upward from the earth. Then, I felt that I was this flame, this chariot of fire, shooting across the night sky. I cried uncontrollably out loud; it felt piercing, raw and sharp. "Oh, she was so beautiful. She is so beautiful . . ." Then, my body or that beautiful fire in the sky began to shed what like bits of charcoal. The pieces flew off my chariot in a gust of wind and dispersed into the galaxy. Then, they were gone; so was I — so was she.

    There was no way to analyze what had just happened except to know that what I had experienced was unexpected, so very real, and now witnessed by another. A couple hours later, I was sitting warm and safe on my grandmother's recliner, which I inherited when she passed last year at ninety-three. I'm working, teaching college, typing, feeling content with my work, my life in general. And then, as I sometimes do, I told Angeles out loud with no one around in my living room, "I'm ready now." "I'm finally ready to work on our project together." This may seem strange but we were so connected spiritually that I would speak to her spirit sometimes. I had realized that I wasn't ready before to research and write this project. I needed to slow down and really savor and enjoy life; that's why I had sought therapy. I needed to breath and fully feel the beauty of my soul and spirit, pure and light, dancing free, both in a vast dark night sky and the glowing light of day.

The phone rang. "Are you sitting down," she asked.

"Angeles Arrien passed away on Thursday." She started to read the announcement on the web page but I couldn't make out the words. All I felt was the shock, terror, empty sadness, and a maddening, raging disbelief that she was gone.

I ran outside into the warm spring afternoon, said I couldn't talk, I needed time. Oh no, my Angeles, how could she have gone and left me here. No! No! No!

I frantically called her office but there was no answer. I left a desperate message for someone to please call me back. I wandered from room to room in my house, looking for solace and peace. I sat down on the couch in front of my ancestor shrine, with my grandmother, my father and yes, a picture of Angeles already there. Why had I placed her photo there just a few weeks before? I had called her three weeks prior to schedule a phone call to talk about project. I didn't hear back which was so unlike her, but I tried to rationalize that she was busy at a conference or retreat. Yet, in the last week, I had started to check her website, for some kind of news or announcement. I was looking for something but I didn't know what. I had pushed away thoughts that something bad had happened. I was grief stricken beyond belief but not surprised. Unlike others, deep down, I had known what the silence meant. I just didn't want to listen. The mind can play powerful tricks over spirit. Now, believe me, I was listening.

I was able to find out that afternoon that the news of her passing had hit the Internet faster than calls could be made. Although I was looking for answers, I knew at once that for me she would never be gone. As I stared at her picture next to Papa, I said out loud, "There is no separation between life and death." She would live in me as my father did. And I would do exactly as I had promised her I would.

In the days that followed I heard a voice inside myself but coming from somewhere else in the kitchen, telling me not to worry that "everything I needed, I already had." Was the message referring to the manuscript I had written called *The Seven Pathways: A Universal Journey into Basque Mysticism*, where she had written the foreword, but we had never heard back from her agent, so had let it go for the a time. When she told me I had everything I needed, was she referring to the translation project on Basque Mysticism we had planned to collaborate on together in the upcoming fall? It was now spring and fall was not far away. How could I possibly begin to imagine starting this project without her? The very thought of it was bittersweet and so uncertain now, but I quickly found my grounding in this uncertainty, as I had come to find a peace in the uncertain space between two worlds having lost Papa through his disappearance. So, during the few days and weeks after she passed, I felt closer to her than ever. I felt her in the gust of wind that would sporadically circle around me when outside under the trees, or new flashes of insight about the project that would speak to me from the oak trees in the forest on my walks behind my house. She would tell me that this project on Basque Mysticism isn't about her. I don't need "her" for this project. It is about the messages that she carries forth, living or passed. She is nature. She is wind. She is tree and forest and sky.

She, Mother Earth, is Goddess Mari, the Goddess Mari that lives in that cave in Bidarrai (Bidarray). Mari is a spirit of feminine gender who predates the Christian era and her characteristic features reflect the prehistoric goddess of death and regeneration. Mari is called "the lady" (of Muru, of Aketegi [Aktegui], of Anboto, etc.), and "the woman." Basque folklore recalls that she was a prophetess who ruled over natural phenomena and guarded moral conduct. She is the vulture goddess, tomb goddess, and regenerator who appears in a multitude of zoomorphic shapes, similar to those she manifested during the Neolithic. The Goddess Mari reflects a complex set of symbols and metaphors related to the birth-death-rebirth cycle which was at the heart of the Old European religion, as we can reconstruct it. The Bird Goddess presided over the realm of birth and fate in the form of ducks, swans, storks, and other waterfowl; as the Wielder of Death, she found expression in the birds of prey; a source of life and regeneration, she was associated with eggs, and with nonavian forms such as the snake. Coiled and serpentine spirals denote the energetic, life-giving aspect of the Goddess; such spirals are sometimes found as birds' eyes, and can be seen in the horn of rams, which animal is sacred to her.

Mari's habitations are by and large subterranean, in mountainous caves. Mari is the Goddess often associated with these caves; she is known as Mari of the Cave. The Basque Country is mountainous and wild, replete with caves and chasms. Souls of the dead emerge occasionally through winding cave galleries and abysses. Devotees leave offerings to the dead and to the goddess at caves. Mari's powers reflect her connection with death-bringing and regenerative functions. The underworld communicates with the upper world by means of aperture: wells, caves, galleries, and abysses.

The names Mari, Lamia, Lady, or Dame are all used to identify witches in countless legends. These legends often include accounts of Mari imprisoned or disappearing into a forest or cave, or instantly, in the burst of a fireball. It is generally believed that Mari is a beautiful lady and her habitations are richly adorned with gold and precious stones. In the stories of Durango, she appears as an elegantly attired lady, holding a palace of gold in her hands. She wears a red gown in Lescun. In Amezteka (Amézqueta), she appears in the form of a lady seated in a carriage drawn though the air by four horses.

Mari takes on bird form in her subterranean abodes: she flies out of caves as a crow or vulture. The bird of prey (vulture, owl, eagle, or raven) was symbolic of this Bird Goddess in the mode of Wielder of Death. It seems clear that the connection between symbols of bird-of-prey and vulva in the Goddess is evocative of the cycle of formation, destruction, and reformation. Mari is known as a woman with feet like a bird in Garagartza (Garagarza) and seen as a raven in in the cave of Aketegi.

Mari is often associated with other animals than the bird, like the bull, ram, the male goat, the horse, the serpent, and the vulture, all mythical animals of the subterranean world. She is also associated with the goat in Mount Hauza (Auza) in the Baztan Valley and as a lady riding a ram in Zegama (Cegama) and Oñati (Oñate).

Similar to the experience I had the day I hear of Angeles' passing, I learned that Mari is often associated with fire in the sky. Mari is often seen flying through the air as either a fireball or burning flame. She flies in the air from one side to the other of the sky surrounded by fire. There are many legends in Basque mythology describing Mari as disappearing or flying in the sky as a burning flame, such as The Lady of Murumendi in Ormaiztegi (Ormaiztegui) where she disappeared from sight in a burst of flames. She has been seen in the form of a woman shooting out flames in Zaldibia (Zaldvidia), as a woman engulfed in fire, stretched out horizontally in the air, passing through space in Bedoña (a neighborhood of Arrasate-Mondragón), and in the form of a woman trailing a fiery wake, sometimes dragging a broom, at other times chains, depending upon the noise that accompanies her passage in Errezil (Régil). She has been seen passing through the air in the form of a ball of fire in Oñati and Orozko (Orosco) and as a fiery sick in Zegama and Zuazo de Gamboa. In Oñati, Mari is also a tree shooting out flames on all sides.

The Goddess Mari is also often associated with trees, wind, and the sky, all mystical elements of nature in Basque mythology. She is a tree whose trunk resembles a woman; a white cloud, a rainbow, a gust of wind, and in the cave of Bidarrai, she is represented by a stalagmite, an upward growing mound of minerals resembling a human torso. She is a Goddess who travels, moving from place to place every seven years.

Similar to the laminak, Mari upholds law codes. Mari condemns lies, thievery, pride, and boasting, the nonfulfillment of one's given word, the failure to respect others, and the failure to give help to others. These are similar themes to those lessons taught by the laminak. She also rules natural phenomena: hail, unexplained gusts of wind, drought, lightning, and rainstorms and is closely tied to cycles of nature, like the laminak. Mari is associated with the moon. This very important Basque goddess gives us information that previous archeological sources could not provide.

The Goddess Mari, as the leader or queen of the spirit world in many Basque myths, is also the matriarch of her family. Mari's husband is Maju or the male snake Sugaar. It is believed that hail and rainstorms occur when they come together. There are also legends of Mari marrying a young, mortal man from the farm of Burugoena in Beasain, and Mari having seven sons. Then, at other times, she appears as a divinity of several sister goddesses, similar to seven sisters of the Basque Virgin Mary.

The Goddess Mari is also the ancient version of the lamia. Basque folklore is full of references to a type of creature called the lamia or laminak, who, are supernatural beings with human form but have the feet of a chicken, duck, or goat. In legends from coastal Bizkaia, they appear with the bust of a woman or the tail of a fish. There are a number of caves, caverns, grottos, and wells named after the laminak, who are said to live chiefly in such places. Since the lamia are believed to have lived in caves in ancient times, many cave and caverns are named after them. Lamia have also been named after mills, ravines, rivers, springs, pools, and places where they were believed to keep their stones. The laminak resemble the little folk of other European folklore. The interesting difference between the Basque laminak and other spirits is that the Basque little folk are always female. Interestingly, the stories always involve depictions of nature and the natural cycles of life, associated with this female laminak. For example, there are stories of men falling in love or asking to marry a lamia, or beautiful woman. Most frequently, lamia are associated with birth and midwifery.

The laminak occupy a position halfway between nature and culture, retaining something of that duality. They are close to nature in their makeup and yet they possess the power to restore social order. The stories of the laminak offer individual, community, and social behavior and moral codes and structures. Honesty, mutual assistance and reciprocity, the clearly defined egalitarian roles of men and women, childbirth, and lessons on greed and temptations of the lure of sexuality and wealth are common themes among laminak stories. Sometimes, there are legends where the lamia help with work in the field and are offered gratitude offerings of bread, milk, cider, corn, and bacon.

In understanding what nature means to the Basques, what is most important to understand is that the earth (*lur*) is considered to be the mother of the sun and moon. The land and the sky are the two integrated halves of the whole of Mother Earth. The most sacred elements of Basque beliefs about life and death are those that are seldom, if ever, talked about. There is no question that the land holds the greatest treasures, mysteries, and value in the Basque culture. Little is written specifically about the Basque's beliefs about their land because the land is the most sacred element of life. To write about the land would be to write about one's true, inner being. Thus, the land is celebrated through song, dance, work, worship, rituals, and practices in everyday life. What Basque mythology does tell us is that the land is an immense surface. The Basques tell that the earth is vast and limitless, a plane extending in all directions. The surface of the Earth is alive, and mountains are believed to grow just as living beings do.

> *The land (she) is covered by cavities or currents and rivers of honey, and this is where the divinities live. These regions are inaccessible to humans while they live on the surface; but at certain wells or shafts, chasms, and caverns there is access to this domain. In this way, the Basque divinities and the deceased come closer to see us. She holds fabulous treasures.*

The land and nature, like the laminak, are always referred to in the feminine. She is a refuge for the mythical animals. For example, the description of *behigorri*, the Pyrenean red cow, strangely resembles the prehistoric pictures from the caverns, the caves, and the abysses. This speaks to the ancient connections between the Basque people and their land. The land contains the lost treasures in the cavities where the "rivers of honey" flow. An example of this is that the rivers were once believed to be sacred. When there was a drought, after mass, the members of a religious association in the community would submerge an image of a patron saint in the river, asking God for rain.

The land is also believed to be covered by the heavens. She is in direct relation to the sky, sun, and moon (upper world). The sun is the daughter of the land, like the moon is the face of God. The land is also connected with the underworld; as the underworld is seen as the place of the force of earth.

Rituals related to the land are dedicated for the purposes of protection. Rituals protect the property, the buildings, and occupants. The priest blesses the fields: at the time of seeding one makes a cross at the center of the field (arzaioz), and then one sows the corn. The night of Christmas (*gabon*), one burns a fire in the chimney. In Ameskoa, for the Saint-Antoine, one brings the cattle to the chapel Saint-Antoine, or makes a circle three times around them. Then, they are blessed.

The land (buildings, house, and property) is a protected space where people and animals live together in the *etxekoak*. These spirits of the underworld manifest to man thru the intermediary of gulfs/abysses or caves, under the appearance of an animal. The sub-terrain or underworld is the residence of the deceased and the divine.

Thus, it is not surprising to see, that man is not seen as an individual in the ancient Basque spiritual tradition. He is seen rather as an integrated part of the land. The spirit world of the individual is an integrated part of the physical world in the ancient Basque Country. All parts of the ancient Basque world were seen as one. And the Goddess Mari is the queen of this sacred land. She/the earth has special gifts that the world needs more than ever before.

Lesson 4

The lesson here, my beautiful children, is to focus on the positive, not the negative, and the positive will grow. See the best in yourself and others. Always be true to your voice, to your truth. Be aware of all the side of yourself, both the sun (light) and moon (shadow). Actively listen to what is needed in the world to regain balance and care enough to make it happen. Be a lighthouse of inner beauty and peace that illuminate your life dream to help others find their own.

5
The Way of the Village

> *"The sounds of the morning, of cocks crowing in a nearby farmyard, of church bells tolling in the village below, of a multitude of birds filling the air with song; sweet perfume from forever blooming trees, air as soft and sensual as a child's caress, white morning mists obscuring the mountains until the sun lifts the veil to reveal green mountains."*
> — Robert Laxalt, *The Land of My Fathers*

Tuesday, July 16, 2015

It poured all day long so we couldn't go horseback riding as we had hoped. The children didn't argue all day long with no Internet and cheesy French shows on TV! We played a card game called "liar liar" that Beñat taught us sitting on the floppy red couch in the front room of our house. I felt like a kid again for the first time in forever, playing games, laughing at nothing, and having fun, mostly laughing at me acting ten instead of forty-three. I'm ok with that. It's a rarity for the children to see me so free and light, no worries about the demands of daily life, work, paying bills, scheduling who picks up who from what practice at what time each day. I suppose on that day I realized how much more peaceful our home life back in California could be if I was always this relaxed and if I gave my children all the attention they want, but this is not realistic. Life has demands and adults have responsibilities.

The misty mountains of Baigura

There was one worry lurking in my mind on this day, a request I didn't feel comfortable about on many levels. Although sometimes it was difficult to speak my truth back home in the states, decisions came to me instantly here. How is it that when I'm on Basque soil, I have such clarity that I don't always have back home? Perhaps it's this place and perhaps it's slowing down. I remember Angeles used to always say that nature's rhythm is medium to slow yet most of us live our lives in the fast or fast to medium range. I wondered how slowing down helps us to be more honest with ourselves and others.

I explained to my friend Diane later that evening as we drank tea at her kitchen table talking for hours like we always do, that it felt good to have a backbone. She said that this place has given her one too. Others had noticed it in her and I could see what she was talking about. She has a visible strength and a surety in her decisions that I respect. Before I went to bed that night, just before the sun was setting, the misty rain still lingering in the air I could feel the anxiety rise in my chest. It isn't easy to set clear boundaries knowing that others will be displeased with your decision or actions.

With the panic welling up in my chest, I darted out of the house and into the main street, the center fo the village (*au bourg*), crossing over to the path to Laka, the river that runs through Ortzaize. I found myself standing in the middle of the poplar trees as the wind swirled fiercely around me, lifting me up inside. I had the sensation in my body that I have had for years when I am dreaming, that I'm flying, high above the earth in the dark night sky with brilliant bright stars encircling me. In these flying dreams, I am lucid. I can control how high I fly, how far I go into the expansive endless sky. I feel weightless and free and with this freedom I fight back fear, fear of flying too high so that I can't find my way back or fear of the unknown that lurks ahead in the vast openness of space. I opened my eyes and felt my feet planted on the ground. The excitement of the whirling wind pulsing through my body like lightning and the loud hum of the trees brushing up against each other startled me and woke me from this daydream. I felt Papa's spirit, Angeles' spirit, and all the spirits of my ancestors holding me up. I felt so strong and clear and grateful for the strength unlocked inside of me. Life throws unexpected stones or "curve balls" back in the states, but within me I have the power to do what is right, what is good, to speak and act with unity and wisdom, always with the ancestors around and within me, protecting me through this mystical journey of life. I hear the words of Terexa, "Within you lies the story; within you lives the folklore."

I am instantly taken back to the day of Angeles's passing, how I danced so freely in my living room for the first time in a very long time. I remembered now that just a few days later, after Angeles passed, I jotted down notes of what she had taught me over the years-seven lessons from the ancient *etxe*. I was afraid I would forget and if I forgot, she would be lost to me forever. Amazingly as I wrote this book, these seven lessons integrate in a seamless tapestry with her own work from *The Four-Fold Way*.

The Way of the Warrior is to show up and choose to be present. How had I not been present with my children before this trip? How had I pushed them away in my business, a business that kept me from facing the pain of life, of caring for a mother with many needs, of trying to distance myself from the responsibilities that burdened me? How had I found such clarity, boundaries, and an inner balance simply by slowing down and playing cards all day in the rain with my two beautiful children? Then, a flash of memory from the dream from July 2014, three months after she passed, blinds me in this forest of poplar trees:

> *I had waited patiently for months and nothing. So often when you were alive, I would dream of you, as my teacher, sitting in the mountains, passing on your wisdom in words that now fill the silence in an empty room. In the dream, you, your sister, whom I've never met and myself are standing in a circle looking in, our three faces are hidden. Then, you say, quickly, firmly and clearly, "You will have to guide them to the Four-Fold Way."*
>
> *I wake up. That's it! Are you serious? Just that one sentence! What does that mean? I haven't studied the Four-Fold Way, except in reading your bestselling book and of course the years of modeling, what I now see was also a way of parenting, you gave so generously to me.*

I had to come all the way for this dream to make perfect sense. Here now as I write, unclear of which path to take, you're telling me to once again, *listen to the ancestors and go back to the village.*

Courageously, go with your heart wisdom, that Basque heart wisdom that has never failed you. She had wanted me to be so successful, to be known for the untapped gifts she saw in me. And for that Angeles, I am grateful beyond the moon and stars, the sun and sky.

But it was and is our trust in the Great Mystery that is the core essence of our connection. You trusted that I would find the way after you transitioned. You trusted that I would carry forth the messages of this Basque spirit we share.

June 17, 2015

My cousin Jeanine picks us up about nine in the morning. In her car, Beñat asks me: "Mom, where are we going again?" I know he's thinking where is she taking us now. I repeat to him, for the third time, "We're going to hike to Harpeko Saindua with Jeanine. Remember, I told you, about the legend of the Goddess Mari and how she is believed to be found in a prehistoric cave in the mountains above Bidarrai."

There is a story behind every story and this is the story of Harpeko Saindua, the sweating sainting, in the cave of Zelharburu deep mountaintop of Arzamendi, the mountain of the cave bear, in Bidarrai.

Eleven Years Ago, in the Summer of 2004

For the past three years I have had numerous dreams that I am flying and soaring through the sky high above the ground. With each gust of wind, I feel like I'm reaching greater heights and watch my fear of flying dissipate into nothing in the open air. As we hiked up the narrow and steep path on the mountaintop in Bidarrai to find the cave of Harpeko Saindua, I felt like doing anything but flying. I wanted to go back to the safe plateau below where I didn't see the steep cliff to my left and the deep mountain ranges and canyon that circled below, to my right.

I have always had a fear of heights. Never before would I even consider hiking such a trail. When my sister would dangle her toes off a mountain cliff on summer vacation, I would stay back in the distance, watching her in awe, but I had wanted to visit this one cave on my trip. Angeles had suggested that I look to the caves for deeper insights and understanding for the final pages of my book. I trusted her guidance and told my cousin Peio, when he asked me what I wanted to see on this trip, about my desire to visit this cave, just a short drive from Ortzaize.

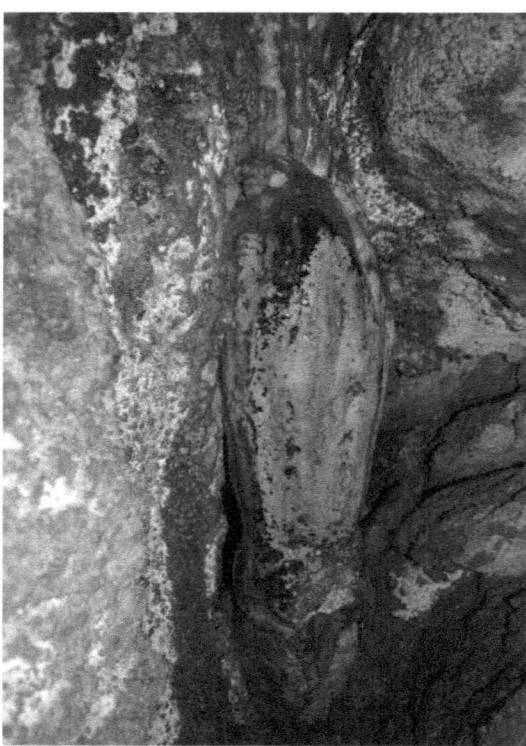

Stalactite believed to represent the Goddess Mari, Harpeko Saindua (cave of the sweating saint), Bidarrai

Harpeko Saindua is the cave of the sweating saint. The water on the stalactite, which looks strangely human in form, is applied to a diseased part of the body and allegedly has curative powers, particularly for the skin. There is a legend that the stalactite from this cave represents the ancient Goddess Mari of rebirth and regeneration. When you see her, you can understand why pilgrims and locals have been visiting this magical site for centuries.

> *The prehistoric cave had the same functions of the etxe today. Like cave, like the house, was a place of work, a temple, and a gravesite.*

The prehistoric origins of the *etxe* are from a cave. The prehistoric Basque man lived in a hut made of branches and sheepskin. The cave was a workshop where tools and diverse instruments were made; it was a graveside where the cadavers of generations of families were buried; it was a temple where engravings, paintings, and sculptures were created, part animal and part human.

These signs and symbols from the Basque cave trace the ancient Basque belief system about life and death — mostly that the house is the extension of the earth — *ama lur* (mother earth) and she (the etxe) is always listening to the messages from the subterranean world. Today, people can visit these famous ancient caves in the Basque Country, such as Izturitze (Isturiz), Leitza (Leiza), Santimamiñe, Sara (Sare), and Zugarramurdi.

I have heard the story about how my Amatchi had even taken her firstborn, my uncle, to this cave as a young boy to cure this eczema, but I had no health problems. I was just driven by my desire to follow the right path set forth by my mentor. But I worried, as with each step I could see how dangerous this

Beñat hiking to Harpeko Saindua on Arztamendi (cave bear mountain)

climb might be for my cousin Peio who was carrying Beñat, not even two years old, on his shoulders, my daughter Delaney and Peio's son Xan, both just four years old. As we continued to climb the mountain, I could see that the four year olds weren't afraid this massive descent to the canyon below, while I, a grown woman, was crippled in fear.

There was a moment when I saw the cave at the top of the mountain and stopped. I could not take one more step. My cousin Peio looked back at me and motioned for me to continue walking. If it had been anyone else, I probably wouldn't have listened and retreated to the safe resting spot below. Without looking to my left where the cliff dropped off, I kept putting one foot in front of the other. When we finally reached the cave, there she was, glistening in the dark womb of her cave.

As I walked toward the womanly shaped sweating stalactite, my daughter's hand tight with mine, I turned to my cousin and said, "But I don't have any health problems."

"Your fears Denise," was all he had to say.

Instantly, I leaned forward with my left hand and lightly touched my fingers to the glowing wet body hidden inside the cave's womb. Without thinking, I rubbed the liquid that seeped from what looks like the back of a woman to the middle of my forehead. The water felt tingly on my skin and awakened something sleeping in my soul. I walked out of her darkness into the light of day. There was only one brief moment as I walked down the mountain that I felt afraid. I was afraid to look down to see how far I had traveled, how high I had soared. But I did look back this time and the view was breathtaking and miraculous. From then on, it seemed like seconds, not minutes or hours, before I reached the bottom of the trail.

I remembered how just two weeks ago, while living in the states, I carried with me such anxiety about everything I did in my everyday life. I was fearful of driving, of leaving my children alone for just a minute for fear of abduction, and most of all, fearful that if I didn't try to control everything around me, it would fall apart. Deep down, I was afraid of heights because I was afraid to fly. I was afraid to leave the ones I love behind and more petrified that they would leave me again. This fear kept me hostage and permeated every cell in my blood, so that I wasn't so afraid to die, because in many ways that would bring me closer back to him; it was that I never fully had the courage to live.

Then, seven massive vultures weaved a circle above her temple cave. Just behind her mountain, the cave bear of Artzamendi once proudly claimed its territory. Now extinct in this region, the cave bear had once been revered by the Basques as a guardian spirit, showing us that all beings created are one and united within this great universe.

I smiled from ear to ear. I put my hands in the air and kissed the sky with God. I laughed inside myself just thinking of what Angeles would think once she heard this story. The Goddess Mari teaches us we must walk through our fears, not run from them, touch the mysterious darkness of her womb even when we feel lost and afraid, and most important, listen to courageous message of the cave bear. That message is to awaken to your own life purpose by creating your own legacy of cave art. Leave your mark.

All I can do now is pray that I will never forget to fly. I can try with all my strength to hold on to courage, which is the absolute opposite of fear. If I hold on as tight to this Basque spirit and wisdom that encircle me now, each day will be a miracle. My life purpose is just as I had written years before in my journal-to share the wisdoms of the Basques in order to be able to inspire others, above all my family. I know this with a trust and faith filled with unspeakable gratitude. It is with this gratitude, that I appreciate deeply the blessings of Mother Earth, cave bear, man, woman and child. I find the patience to wait for her multitude of blessings to unfold, with each step, in my life.

Eleven Years Later

It has rained hard the night before so the ground was muddy and slick. Beñat took the lead, walking briskly with his black Nike backpack carrying our bottled water and probably his cell phone that had no reception here in France, but kept it anyway to play video games and take ridiculous, silly pictures of his mother dancing around the living room, making funny faces and gestures to make him laugh. Delaney walked with me, a bit more cautious than her brother; she carefully watched her footing and held on to the ropes when she could. I had remembered the mountain being so much steeper. Today, the climb to Harpeko Saindua seemed to pass quickly and easily, except for the very last climb up the muddy steps to the cave. Yet, I wasn't afraid at all. My children are strong but careful, smart, and brave. I'm proud of them. They didn't complain once. I think they were curious. After all, for years they have seen the pictures of the Goddess Mari in this cave hanging on my office wall, a picture that shows all the bright colors of grey, pink, and golden outlining her figure, with a coin hidden in the stones. When we finally did reach the cave, it was darker than I remember, especially the back of the cave where Mari lives. Delaney turned on her cell phone to use the flashlight and followed Jeanine up three muddy steps. I watched Delaney reach her arm out to find Mari's sweating back. I called out for her to put it on her skin and make a wish. The wish was my additional request. Maybe it comes from throwing pennies in water wishing wells, or maybe it's because eleven years ago, Mari had granted my wish to not be afraid.

After Delaney was Beñat. Once inside her dark womb, he whispered to me, "Mom, did you find that coin in your picture?" (He had been paying attention). Then, with bright eyes he called out, "Mom, I can hear the mountain breathing. It's alive." "Yes, Beñat, she is alive. Now, make a wish but don't tell me what you wish for."

After a few moments, he quietly walked away and I entered, so excited to see her again. I held my hand out in the darkness, finding wet body. Then, without thinking, I instantly touched my forehead, heart, and both cheeks, making the sign of the cross without realizing it. I mumbled under my breath — peace, courage, joy, and love — for myself and for her.

Beñat and Delaney were extra quiet as we slowly found our way back to the car parked in front of the house at the entrance. I could see they were deep in thought. I could tell they were touched by this experience. After that day, Beñat stopped teasing me about searching for Basque Mysticism. When I won a card game, or made a basket on the court, when someone showed up just when I was looking for them, when the mist from the mountain cleared when we needed to see where we were going, he said nothing. "That was cool Mom," was all he said out loud, but for twelve years old, what more can I ask for? I knew what he meant. I knew what he saw. I knew what he felt. I knew what he heard in that cave-the beating of a heart, the pulse of a mountain, the slow and steady breathing, inhaling and exhaling, of a woman giving life back.

June 18, 2015

When I am in pain and I need to find that special place in my mind to escape into peaceful meditation, I can now go back to this vision etched in my memory. I'm on a big white horse on top of the mountain range in Ortzaize. I can see my daughter sitting up straight and proud, tapping her feet on the side of her grand dark horse, to move faster up the windy dirt path up the mountain. I can feel the wind slowly and lightly brushing across my arms, back and cheeks as I close my eyes in complete awe at the magic of riding with prehistoric horses, gazing over farms scattered in the village below, many of them owned by my relatives for generations. I feel the sense of oneness with this mystical place, both free and detached galloping on the horse, and grounded to the ancestral soil beneath me. To say the view is breathtaking doesn't tell the whole story. To my right, there is the village of Irisarri (Irissarry), dotted red roof tops on high mountaintops and deep expansive valleys; to my left is Ortzaize and then past that, the village of Baigorri (Saint-Étienne-de-Baïgorry) whose mountain range extends almost all the way to the border of Spain. I could even see the partially restored roof of the mill house nestled among the trees and prairie. I breathe and close my eyes, taking in the sensation of the cool mountain air and the visions of villages below in my mind, storing them for later when I may need a reserve of strength and calm. I think to myself how I could walk this horse all day, so relaxed, almost hypnotic, until I wake up the next morning and I can barely move. Every bone in my body feels jolted out of place and muscles are sore that I didn't know I had! But the horseback riding adventure was worth every second of the pain, just as every pain in life has been worth every joy that has come after.

June 19, 2015

The next morning, the sun shines once again as I sit outside the gite on the patio drinking my coffee, gazing peacefully at Baigura Mountain. Delaney prepares to cook the noon meal of appetizers before the main dish of *piperade*, sausage and fries. She has started cooking on this trip for the first time and actually makes most of our main noon meals. What a pleasure and relief it has been to not cook every day and to see this young lady find her independence maneuvering about the kitchen. Thinking back to our magical day on the mountain range with the horses yesterday and then seeing her cook dinner through the open patio doors, I am sure that this trip has been for my children. I've traveled here every few years since I was twenty-three years old, but since we moved back from living here for two years from 2010 to 2012 to start restoring the mill house, the children have started to lose some of the innocence of their childhood, and it bothers me. They are so glued to technology that I wonder how they are socially developing. When I try to tell them that when I was growing up we just had one landline phone, they can't believe it. "How did people know where you were and how to get a hold of you?" They seriously ask, as I hold back laughter. "They didn't," I reply. You just had to wait until there was phone available. Being here, we are so much more in sync with the rhythms of everyday life with community and nature, following our own natural instincts and our hearts desire. We take our time to talk slowly with friends and family without interruption. Although, in the last five to ten years, the youth, and even adults, have become more attached to technology, and it worries me. How much will the use of technology take away from the essence of Basque life that honors a pace that is, as my mentor Angeles said, medium to slow. If the pace speeds up too quickly, what parts of the ancient culture will be lost? These thoughts arise as the sun shines above the mountain range in the bright blue sky with dotted white clouds on this lovely summer morning, instill in me a desire to pass on all that I know about the best parts of this place to my children. They will need these lessons in life, when they venture out on their own to college, when they search for a job, when people disappoints them, and they will, when there is pain, and there will be, they can close their eyes, remember the view from the top of that mountain range, where they galloped alongside prehistoric horses, peeking down at their ancestral home, and know where they have come from. I want my children to know their lives matter; who they are matters most, their inner most being, their spirits. That is probably what the Basque Country has taught me most, that my being and their beings are a part of a larger cycle of seasons that pass each year without fail, from generations and generations before me, that have been born in their house and returned there after they're gone.

The spirit of the Basque people is interconnected with nature. Love of nature is central to romantic love and love of family, home, and community. My father wrote his deep connection and love of nature in this courtship letter to my mother:

I hear the wind blowing outside. It reminds me of my country. Especially during the fall there was a wind coming from the south which could make beating my heart. I knew the doves will come crossing over mountains toward the Spain, and I could feel the wind, so strong, so close to the ground. It's nice to remember those wonderful moments. I have no doubt of our love as I relate to the times of the past. I am so romantic sometimes that I get lose in those events to which I have been involved during my youth. But there is something else I loved, which makes me love those feelings even now; that is the wild nature. I was young then, nothing to worry about. My home was swarm, my parents whole. My family was good to me. But as they were sleeping after a hard day of work, I happened to get up from the bed and go to the window for breathing. The good aroma of the night; you could hear the small animals, the ewe call and sing "cris cris," and the smell of nature. I like staying there just watching the stars and moon sometimes during those hours long. And I was happy. And now the only moments I am so happy are when being with you. Believe me. I am ready to love you more than anybody else in the world. Perhaps you find funny that I write you this way, but I would like so much someone who would share every sentiment running into my blood and my heart.

June 20, 2015

I woke up early staring at the wooden ceiling beams in my bedroom, with the windows partially opened to let the fresh air into the warm room. I wake up with intense, clear thoughts here, as if I'm not fully awake from the night before's dream. I realize that the two conflicts I have had here were both tied to the *etxe*, not just the physical structure, but the house's symbolic meaning. Serendipitously both conflicts were about one person refusing to stay with another in their house (me refusing the family member to stay with me; my aunt upset that I didn't stay with her). Both of these conflicts for me were about trust and freedom. The *etxe* must be a free and honest place. One must be able to honestly and freely express themselves in every way they feel comfortable. The home is the birthplace of honest free expression. When the Basques were oppressed by Franco and couldn't speak Basque outside the house, they kept the language alive inside their homes. The folklore of the Basque people is embedded in the mystical path of everyday life events that revolve around the *etxe* and its direct connection to the community or village. Having this illumination sends chills up my spine for I trusted that by coming back here to Papa's homeland and now my homeland in the Basque Country, I would find all the information I need to complete this project. Even more miraculous is the process is the outcome and the outcome in the process. What I mean by this is that with each breath I take and each encounter I have as I put one foot in front of the other, the Great Mystery unfolds in its perfect timing. I have done nothing but show up and be present. Angeles knew the principle that guides the Warrior in indigenous societies is to "Show up and Choose to be Present!" Pay attention to the synchronicity in everyday life and all that is happening both within and outside of you, in your environment and with all your relations. I feel Angeles smiling this bright Saturday morning in June as the rooster crows and the church bells toll. This book has been invisibly writing itself. Life invisibly writes itself. Death invisibly writes itself. We are authors of this book. We are messengers of our story. We are change makers, but there is an invisible hand that guides us to our destiny.

The *etxe*, as the center of Basque Life, is always teaching us this, even in the smallest, most unremarkable ways. For instance, the Internet connection in this vacation rental hasn't worked very well at all; it's extremely slow and spotty. Every day it has tested my deepest patience, forcing me to slow down and not get frustrated. I breathe in deeply, stretch, and try to relax as I wait for the connection bar to reach full capacity on my wireless router. As maddening as this is, the character attribute that I have definitely struggled with the most in my life is patience. I am by nature not a patient person and I know that. Angeles knew that and she constantly guided me through modeling toward the positive aspects of slowing down. I can still hear her say to me, the last day we visited, "You are so busy, Denise." Although I didn't want to admit it, she was right, I was so busy, too busy. Business can be a distraction from facing hardship in one's life, enjoying the present, and living one's life dream.

Lesson 5

Your dreams will manifest in time if you (1) never give up on what you believe in and believe in something larger than yourself, (2) trust in the process and be patient, (3) realize you're never alone, (4) focus on the positive and the positive will grow, and (5) embody these wisdoms in your daily life and in all your interactions by protecting your health, home, and family first. Only then will your life dream manifest and the Warrior within you will lead others to follow—because of who you are. Follow your true nature as Nature is a self-fulfilling prophecy—what you put into it is what you get out of it.

You have the capacity to either see the best or the worst of the world. If you see and believe the best in yourself and others, you will manifest that within yourself. The village and community help you be your best self by identifying your strengths and supporting their development. By having positive beliefs, you are more likely to act and behave in positive ways. Others then respond to these actions and behaviors in more positive ways to you.

This feedback loop is a self-fulfilling prophecy. In nature this happens all the time. When a plant is given sunlight and water and the right conditions for planting, it grows and flourishes, but when it is not cared for it withers and dies. The positive feedback loop of the Way of the Universe, or the blue ring of life, is an ongoing and cyclical process that strengthens the community.

This continuous, interconnected blue ring of life of the village is about learning and relearning: about continually letting go and actively becoming part of a larger circle of relationships. These relationships include all beings, great and small, alive and deceased. A significant part of learning to live fully within this great web of life is being able to give and receive within your circle of supports (your family, friends, neighbors, village, or community).

The word for this give and take is mutual reciprocity. There are strong traditions of reciprocity in the Basque village, as seen in birth, death, and bereavement rituals. There is a deep innate human desire to be part of community. Being part of community helps us to fully realize our life purpose. The need to belong, receive, and give support is basic to human survival. The village helps one find their life purpose and meaning within the context of the larger community and neighboring communities. Friends, relatives, and neighbors help you realize this purpose and meaning by honestly telling you what you need to hear, and showing and guiding you to the next phase of life. You learn how to live in harmony with community by sharing your gifts. This act of giving of your unique gifts and talents helps to reclaim your inner peace and balance and the balance of the entire community.

This Basque Village, in constant relation with the perennial wisdoms of Nature and Mother Earth, teach compassionate service, and mutual reciprocity within the community, a shared experience of give and take. The land is a mirror, reflection, and primary source of inspiration to reawakening and grounding oneself to the wisdom of nature's seasons and cycles. The sky serves as a practical guide for following the cycles of the seasons and as inspiration for innovation and creativity. It provides direction for hunting and gathering and offers signs and omens related to ancestor spirits. Nature is the bridge of inspiration and connection between self, family, and village/community. In this respect, the village and the land are places of belonging, protection, stability, security, and freedom. The land is the provider and supplier of health and abundance in the Ancient Basque World as daily survival (farming, fishing) is dependent upon successful integration.

> *"Throughout history, men and women who have explored the way of the Warrior have been leaders, protectors, sorcerers, adventurers, and explorers." — from Angeles Arrien,* **The Four-Fold Way**

The balanced relationship of mutual reciprocity nurtured in the self and others through an exchange of goods, services, and assistance is tied to health. Cultures worldwide have long understood that listening to and have a connection with the village or community, and nature is critical for health. Indigenous people believe that health and wellness is an alignment and balance of mind, body, and spirit: action/deeds (physical), words and thoughts (mental), and feeling (emotions and spiritual). All parts are interrelated and interdependent, holistic, and nonlinear/circular in nature. This spiritual self is expressed in practical ways, through the everyday activities of life and living balancing out hard work and tenacity, and patience and listening. It requires trusting one's intuition and gaining for and allowing the reception of trust from others. It means being loyal to one's word and showing this loyalty through action. Having congruence and alignment between, thought, word, and deed shows the highest level of honor and respect in the Basque culture.

Give your gifts to those in your village and receive the gifts they bring. This will bring you balance and harmony. Through sharing your creative expression in the community, new insights and illuminations of your life purpose and meaning will emerge.

Leave your unique imprint on the cave wall.

6
The Way of Two Worlds

"Heaven and Earth have always been ours to embrace. The Dream is not just a Mystery of the night; it is the promise of a new day. It is our choice to live Under the Sun — to shine our light, to change our world-the same way, she changed mine."
— Excerpt from a poem written to my late maternal grandmother after her passing

Later that afternoon, the mill house whispers this message to me, gently and sweetly nudging me to move forward with her restoration. This is my second trip to the mill with my uncle and godfather, Jean-Pierre already in the two weeks of this trip. He has clearly taken a special interest in helping me with the mill house this time. Before my arrival, he mowed and cleared a waling path around the mill house and cabin, and pruned the overgrown shrubs and vines. There is no doubt he had intended to take me here, to show me the damage of the July 4, 2014 flood that took one life, a miller; ruined many homes, businesses, and roadways; and is still being repaired a year later. This wasn't the first, nor would it most likely, be the last flood to hit the mill house. Jean-Pierre had built me a lovely golden walking bridge when they brought me here for the first time in the summer of 1993. The next year a flash flood wiped it completely out.

He drove me around the parameter of the three-acre field near the mill to show me how far the water had risen. The ride was rather quiet. Neither one of us had much to say. Most everything between us had been said or at least understood. He is a man who weighs his words carefully and thinks before speaking. I felt awkward in my body, a bit tense and frozen, as I often do around him and other older Basque men. It has nothing to do them and everything to do with me. I never had one of these Basque fathers, at least not in my physical presence. When we arrived at the gate, I offered to open it, but eighty-three-year-old Jean-Pierre, tan, lean, muscular, leaped out of the torn cloth truck seat with the energy of a schoolboy and quickly pulled upon the tired and tattered wooden gate.

At the old Mill House gate

Miraculously, the mill house remained untouched from the fierce flood, except for the kitchen area where stacked wood and old mill parts had fallen into a massive heap of disarray onto the floor. I followed him cautiously inside, running past a family of bats that had taken refuge here in the past three years since we moved back to California. He looked me at inquisitively, as if he couldn't begin to understand my fear of bats. He strolled, slowly and relaxed, past them like they were little blue birds welcoming us home. We had lived two different lives, in two different worlds.

After we walked inside and around the mill house, I followed him outside to the stack of wood pilings and leftover red roof tiles from three years ago when Chad refinished a part of the roof. The main room of the mill remained open to the elements, with massive wooden beams, hundreds of years old, tilted downward, ready to drop into the canal below. It seems almost everyone in the village felt the weight of these wood beams falling, because each time any mention of the mill entered conversation, a villager would say how sad it is that the roof isn't finished. I always had excuses, but the Basques don't like to hear excuses. They are people of keeping your word with actions.

The mill house has not been lived in in over forty years. The last person to live here was a man named Gill who repaired bikes. We still find old steel and iron bike parts and remnants in the creek bed from time to time. Before Gill, was a young family who lived here. I believe the young father worked for my uncle and was tragically killed in a work-related truck accident. Then, there is the story I happened to find out about one afternoon as I rode bikes with my cousin in the village. We stopped to chat with an old woman who told me she grew up in the mill. Her parents both died very young from respiratory infections or the flue. She thought the dampness of the mill and all the dust and flour was not good for their lungs. She and her two siblings were orphaned one dark, cold winter and went to live with their aunt who raised them. Standing over the stack of building materials, hearing the constant humming of the creek to the right and gazing upon the sacred mill walls of sturdy stone and lush ivy, I couldn't help but fight back these flood of memories about the mill and how even today, only stone walls and fallen wood beams, it still speaks its story. Jean

Pierre spoke. He had a suggestion and it was only a suggestion, he noted, for Chad and I would have to decide what we felt is best for the mill, but he had an idea. Perhaps, David, his grandson, my cousins' youngest son, who has his own carpentry business, could restore it. He, his son Peio, and other family members could all help to save money and David would give me a good price, he was sure of it. Synchronically, Chad and I had already discussed this idea before our trip.

"Très bonne idée," I quickly replied, looking him in the eye. And that was that.

It was never a decision to rebuild the mill house after that summer in 1994 when I came here all alone as a young woman.

Summer 1994

I'm walking over shaky stones and boulders and trying not to lean so far to my

left or right that I will succumb to the trembling in my feet, and fall to the ground. I keep repeating out loud to myself in a whisper, not even the trees can hear, "how could this be mine?" I carefully push aside wiry tangled silver branches that have taken over our old eighteenth-century mill house and petite isle, the small island that we have inherited, nestled on the bank of a stream that flows into the Errobi (La Nive), the river that flows between the Pyrenees Mountains from France to Spain, in the lowland valleys of the Basque Country.

I have to stop and breathe because my body is too full with wonder to stop the tears from gushing down my face. I hear nothing. I don't even feel the cool breeze upon my neck as the sun shines gently over the river's bank. All I know is that someone is speaking to me. I fight the urge to be afraid, for I can sense that if I give in, for just one instant, this voice will leave me.

> *I stop. I see this white, bright light piercing above the tallest shrub that hangs over the west edge of the riverbank. When I turn my head to notice this light, I almost fall off the awkward stones and boulders that make up our petite isle. And then, the voices speak to me. I can feel my spine lock and as I freeze, so does every cell and muscle in my once warm and moving body. First my heart sinks in; then my stomach starts to fall in unison. Then my limbs and joints give in to the awesome gravity of this force that is pulling me out of my own mind, into the light and beyond.*

"Oh my God," I cry and weep and sob. I can't stop myself and I don't want to. I feel like I'm purging someone else's pain and I can't even find the reason why because I am too close to the spirit to even separate myself. My legs tingle with chills and the fresh ocean spray from the river below begins to dry the tears on my face. And then I know, what is happening.

I murmur to myself, "Oh, Papa, how much you must have loved her — how sad it must have been for you to lose her — and us — to watch us grow without you here — to not even have known you — never to have known you. The love you felt for her, the love she felt for you is as strong as this grief. Love and loss are inseparable. The magnitude of one cannot exist without the other."

> *I don't remember walking away. To this day I can't even begin to talk about it without crying. It is the most beautiful and saddest moment of my life. My Papa spoke to me, through me, and somehow, beyond all the questions and mysteries surrounding my father's disappearance, I let go of trying to understand, and for once, I fell into the vast spaciousness between this world and the other.*

After that day, people in the village knew that the mill house was sacred to me. I will never forget the words of a Basque man who told me: "I can tell you are Basque by the way you look at your land." There is a sacred space between the two worlds, integrated with the *etxe* that only exists in the stillness and silence of nature.

Jean Pierre and I slowly made out way back to his very used once white Toyota Tacoma and drove back to Irochbeheria. Marie Jeanne, as tradition goes, offered us a drink on the patio table, beneath the maple tree. After his beer and my citron with water, we both stood up simultaneously, in that somewhat uncomfortable space between action and reflection, words and silence. "Denise, I can see you have a good heart." In other words, I'm helping you because I believe in you, not just because I'm your godfather, or because out of tradition I gave you away at your wedding in California, and left my small village and took my first vacation at sixty-five years of age, to give you away for your father, but because you have earned it; you deserve a helping hand. I have seen how you care for others, how you love everyone in the family, despite the ghosts in the closet, the unresolved and enduring family conflicts, that you are able to move forward, focusing on the best of each of us, instead of our mistakes.

He didn't say any of this of course, but he didn't have to. In the ancient Basque tradition, the wise elders say very little but when they do speak, their words are powerful and meaningful. It is the job of the young to listen deeply to silence in between the words, to the eternal rushing waters of the creek, to the distant winds that wake up forests at night, to welcome to a new day, a bright, morning sun, full of hope and promise. I would wait now for David to help me rebuild the mill once again. For the first time in my life, I could actually see it happening. Maybe, Papa, I will rebuild your mill house after all, maybe then, you can be set free from the two worlds that trap you. Maybe Papa, our dreams will come true.

    Later that evening, around eight, just as the sun begins to slowly descend behind the mountain range, casting its soft glow over the valley, we drove up the windy village road to Irochbeheria. My cousin Peio having apologized earnestly and honestly for not been able to pick us up at the airport wanted to have us over for dinner. We arrived at his "party room," an expansive single room separate from the house with large windows and sliding glass doors on all three sides, two massive long wooden tables with benches that extend the entire length of the room, a full length bar, and a kitchen with a wide *plancha* for grilling. To my surprise, almost the entire family was there to greet us. With white wine in hand, I strolled from cousin to cousin catching up on all we had missed in the three years we had been gone. The children were doing well in school, they were playing sports, Chad was working full-time at the jail, all good news about our lives.

    My cousin Peio and aunt Marie Jeanne were busy at the *plancha* preparing homemade *talos*; flour *talos* carefully prepared from scratch, by hand, in between working at the vineyard, preparing daily soup from her garden, and keeping her eight-bedroom house spotless, my aunt and godmother, at seventy-nine years of age, had squeezed in preparing these amazing homemade *talos*. Peio was grilling the pork from his own pigs. The smell of fresh ham and fat drippings filled the smoke filled room and the aged sheep cheese, a stable in their diet, was thinly sliced and ready to be placed with the ham in the *talo*. Almost all the food at Irochbeheria comes from the farm, except for the bread that gets delivered to their kitchen windowsill and a few items from the local grocery store, such as yogurt, milk, and cheese, although it wasn't too long ago that they milked the cows and pasteurized it right at home on their stove.

As I meandered from cousin to cousin, the children played soccer or "fut" (from "foot(ball)") outside on the grassy field. Later that evening, as the sun set the lights from the church in the village square below illuminated the hillside. The stars sparkled through the windows lightening up the room. The conversations flowed from the latest news of productive activities, from engagements, passing baccalaureate exams, and doing "stages" or internships at local farms and businesses. As the night ticked on, the conversations grew deeper and more intimate as they often do and my aunt began to share with me what it was like growing up here as a young girl. I had told her that I was interested in hearing stories of Papa in his youth before he left for America, but I knew these stories didn't come quickly or easily, or without guarded tears, so I waited patiently. Instead, she told me how as children, for dinner, they were given just a bowl of milk and bread, while her mother, my Amatchi, would save the bread for the children and only have milk, corn, and if it was a luck day, a fresh egg. Her father, my Itachi (grandfather), would have an egg and some jambon, ham, as he needed the protein to work on the farm, herding the sheep and cows, tending the garden and all the daily activities and challenges that went with running a farm in the 1940s chaos of World War II France. What my aunt wanted me to know was that her parents saved the bread for the children. They sacrificed their bread, a symbol of life, so their children could grow and prosper. The message was and is quite simple — there is sacrifice in life and in families. Children come first, family comes first, and the most basic of needs come first. I also sensed that she wanted me and the children to understand the humble beginnings of her and Papa's childhood, that life was very simple then, in some ways much harder than today, but in others easier, because there weren't distractions like smart phones and social media. There was hard work, a dinner shared together after a long day in the sun, and peaceful nights under the sky lit sleeping village. There was no television, no movies, no radio. There were stories around fireplaces. There were baby brothers that died in childbirth and some as toddlers, later to be renamed as my uncle and my father. There were breathing walls in this house, thick walls made of stone that kept generations after generations of family secrets safe.

As the table hummed with chatter, laughter, and clicking wine classes, I leaned over and asked my cousin Peio to sing me a song. "I came all the way from California," I pleased, smiling coyly. My uncle Jean Pierre must of overhead my request and began singing a song, "Txoria Txori," a song well known and beloved throughout the Basque Country.

"Txoria Txori"
Hegoak ebaki banizkio
Neria izango zen
Ez zuen aldegingo
Bainan, honela
Ez zen gehiago txoria izango
Eta nik . . . txoria nuen maite

The bird is a bird
If I had clipped her wings
She would have been mine
She would not have fled
But, thus
She would not have been anymore a bird
And I . . . I loved that bird.

— Lyrics by Joxean Artze and music by Mikel Laboa

Sunday, June 21, 2015: The Summer Solstice

Strolled along the beach in Hendaia (Hendaye), the fishing port between the border of France and Spain. The sandy beach stretches for miles along the shallow shores that slowly deepen into the bright blue green Atlantic sea. The beach is perfect for children and families because it is shallow for hundreds of feet out. Young toddlers in sunhats wearing their tanned birthday suits, make castles in the sand, while young parents watch over them. Delaney and Beñat spend hours riding the waves with boogey boards while I walk the beach from one end to the other.

The three days in Hendaia are a dream. We fall asleep to the sound of waves in the distant port below Evelyne's apartment. No allergies so we breathe easy and we sleep even easier. Beñat tries paella for the first time and loves it so much he orders it every night. Delaney finds the perfect straw hat with long elegant brims to cover her fair skin face. I escape from all the worries back home. These thoughts fade away into the horizon so that I can't recall what bothered me before now.

Lighthouse at Hendaia

But my mind does race back from time to time to our first evening here, when my cousin Jeanine and I walked out on the pier. As we walked along, barefoot in the sand, she pointed to where her father had drowned several years back, just a year and a half after her mothers' untimely death. First my aunt, her mother, then six months later our other aunt Leoni, then a year after that her father. Three tragic, unexpected losses all within such a short period of time. Too much for anyone.

I felt a deep connection with her mother, my aunt, who was very close with my father, being only two years younger than him. I hadn't spent much time with my aunt on this world but I knew her through another one. She had been the first to invite me to write again after years of silence. We were living in Ortzaize in 2010. I remember it was fall because I remember the cool breeze behind my back from the open window. I can still see the dew glistening on the green grass outside the red shudders and the light streaming from the opening in the fluffy white clouds, contrasting to the gray thunder sky lurking behind the lowlands of the Pyrenees Mountains.

I was sitting at Jeannine's kitchen table. To my left, my uncle Jean-Baptiste, to my right, stands Jeannne preparing appetizers. I can see my uncle sitting straight, talking crisp, exact French, telling stories of history only he knew and must share as now, in his eighties, a retired Basque history professor, our special uncle but one of the worlds' most noted and prolix writers on Basque history in Iparralde (the northern or French Basque Country).

We were sharing a casual aperitif. I don't recall the occasion because there are so many reasons to celebrate being together as family, whether it's a holiday, or just a Sunday to connect. The conversation flies from politics to World War I or World War II, so distant for us Americans but not for the French in the Basque Country, who remember hiding Jewish refugees, running from German soldiers on their long walk in the country to the school in the village, to pregnant mothers who were beaten and kitchens barren after the soldiers raided their cupboards, stole their chicken and eggs and left them starving.

Then, there were footsteps from above where Jeanine's sister Evelyn and her family lived. Like many large farm houses in the Basque Country, there are often divided in half where families share a single dwelling. Sometimes the lone aunt or uncle, sometimes the sister or brother, sometimes the parents, live together separated only be a wall but seamless as a family unit.

She entered the kitchen with a journal in her hand and a smile of mischief I knew so well as a Basque woman of faith. Not the kind of faith that is only religious but the kind of faith that is a knowing, a felt knowing that lives so deep and familiar in the bones that it's impossible to separate what the mind and heart understands as truth.

Eyes turned to her, then me as silence filled the kitchen. In French, Evelyn says, "I was cleaning through some old boxes just above you (looking at me), when I came upon this box of my mother's that I had never opened until now. At first when I opened the journal, I thought it was blank but then I looked in the back and turned upside down was this . . ."

My aunt had written in her journal in French, the following: "A letter written by Denise, the daughter of my brother Beñat, after her sole trip to the house of her father." Below this sentence in her journal were the exact words I had written in English, transcribed into French by my aunt:

> I am never afraid of what I know. For me, this phrase explains much of the mysteries of Papa in this country. Each day that I am here, when I am alone, I am never lonely.

When I look at this magnificent country I know that I it is part of me. I am a stranger in a faraway land with a language, values, different faces surround me. But I am never afraid. I walk across this country and a voice tells me: "God lives here!" When I walk on the roads of the village, they stare at me, the old woman on the bench, the men in their cars, but I am never afraid. They whisper and speak of my strange clothes, my American ways and they remember, one more time, the story of Papa.

There are all the stories and all the suffering, all the tears and above all the uncertainty!

But for me there is above all and only the true feeling (or truth) that he is gone. His soul is on heaven. I know, all these things now. My father would never have left his country and his family. His love that I feel here is the love of my father. The courage, the force and the certainty that I feel I know is the same. I will never know the voice of my father, his smile, his laugh and I am profoundly sad when I this of this, the suffering that he left behind. Now I know as certainly as the sun rises and sets that Papa is gone but his memory rests in the free prairie of the country. His courage shines in the magical river that casts its light on the land and his strength is now our strength. I have never been more aware of how much I love life. How blessed I am and how sure I am that God lives here and in me. "Je vows aims rouse taut," and I am not sad, as difficult as this can be, (vaut le coup d'être venue), I am never afraid of what I know."

Chills. Shock. Disbelief. Magic. Her presence here now. My father's presence here now. Us here now. The worlds of seen and unseen as one now. "How did she know this? How did my aunt translate this from English to French?" My aunt had passed away seven years previously and just now; it is found? I had originally written these words in my journal. I had shared it with no one but God. I had found my father and my soul that summer in 1995 before husband and children, after heartache and loss. Alone and afraid I followed my Basque heart back to my father's homeland knowing my family only through two short vacations when I was nine and nineteen, and letters in French at Christmas. That summer had saved me from a misguided path, I'm sure. I had found my roots in a faraway land, so completely different than growing up white in poor rural America with a culture of pop music and designer jeans, a single mom with mental problems, a frightened child, but always smiling and full of hope and courage and strength. It was then that I knew where those came from. It was then that I returned home to find myself, not alone, but one with home, family and nature.

How could she have known these things? Why did she leave them in this journal without any other words but empty spaces to fill? Even if somehow my journal had been discovered and translated into French, the fact that Evelyn had not found this journal until this moment, a moment that had arrived only after having moved my entire family back to France. This moment never would have arrived if I hadn't followed my heart back to the home of my father-again.

I will never forget Evelyn's words . . . In front of everyone at the table, once silent and observant with my struggling French accent, I was now the center of attention.

"This is an invitation Denise." This is an invitation to write again.

Three months later, standing over the kitchen sink of our five-hundred-year-old rented house Tarbenia, I rushed outside, pen and paper, the invisible hand to follow, a poem came instantly and directly to and through me. It is important to understand that the particular route where the living communicate with ancestor spirits arises from the sub-terrain world and enters through the opening of natural cavities, the fireplace, and the mantel in the kitchen. The *etxe* is positioned under the universe where she communicates to the underworld by way of the ducts and in particular, the hearth.

Water and fire are purifying elements used within the *etxe* to clear up bad omens with spirits. The *etxe* is blessed with water and one says: "blessed water conceived from heaven, bless this earth, that which leaves this house, and all bad things." The water collected during the night is used for bad spirits; for the clearing up, one uses a red poker in the fire against the bad omens. It is Erio, the God of the dead, who separates the spirits of the dead and the messenger who wanders in the underworld, where the supernatural forces exist. The spirits are often named *argi* (light). The dead in the underworld return to their *etxe* and follow the canals/ducts, which open in the caves, the abysses, and in the houses.

> "The Invitation"
>
> If I could forgive everyone
> I would.
> If we could just sit and talk, be friends again
> I would.
> If we could just right our wrongs
> Correct all our mistakes
> If we could just leave the past behind us, locked up at last,
> I would.
> If I could just be here now
> With nothing but this love
> I would.
> If I could just stop time
> And start again

> I would.
> If I could change winter into summer
> Fall back into spring
> If I could bring all these souls to life again
> I would.
> But I am just a word, a pen,
> A hand that moves with you.
> I am just a messenger
> Who knows no way but through.

Evelyn said, "In every generation there is someone in the family lineage who is the messenger. She communities the message from the other side. Who has the gift of seeing, as seer; in our family, that is, you."

Many of the old way mystical practices are gone now except to where they may have transmitted it to the first born in their families or to other children who may have had natural propensities for maintaining, or showed gifts surrounding mystical practices. There are few people currently from ages to seventy to ninety who will talk openly surrounding Basque Mysticism, given the Franco regime in Spain and before that so many families being touched by the Spanish Inquisition. There are current revivals surrounding learning the Basque language and the dances in the old ways, which have deep roots in Basque mystical practices. Most Basque Mysticism is embodied rather than talked about or announced.

As I had for the past ten years, I shared these recent events taken place in the kitchen of Xuitenia with Angeles. As always, she, of everyone, knew the significance and profound meaning of what had transpired. Shortly after Christmas, at the beginning of the New Year, I received Living in Gratitude "a la poste" to my front door at our rental home, Tarbenia. Inside handwritten in black ink, it reads: "for Denise, so grateful to have you in my life-with love, gratitude and admiration to you always — Miss you, Angeles."

Angeles knew that my return to the Basque Country was an ancient, but contemporary rite of passage. There was no other way to be acknowledged for one's natural gifts without the confirmation from one's family in the homeland. I had re-ceived validation in the past from other cousins as I first shared my dissertation on Basque Spiritualism and later my integra-tion of The Seven Pathways.

"How do you know these things, Denise?" Evelyn and Jeanine asked me. "You grew up in California so far away and distant from this land, yet you know, see and understand as-pects of the ancient Basque Ways that are even hidden now from those born and raised here."

I have come to understand on a deeper level that Papa's mysterious death and the absence of his physical presence in my life has heightened my intuitive knowing and "seeing." His mys-terious death had opened my spirit up to the mysteries of life.

As Jeanine and I strolled along the pier, the conversation the turned to Papa, as I suspected it would. Here, forty-two years later, we're still talking about his disappearance. I could feel my breath tighten and my body ache but I held strong as I placed one foot in front of the other, wind blowing from the sea. The pier seemed to stretch on for days. The slow pulse of time ticking away, tick-tick-tock, the story never changes. I had heard this story before, about how my aunt, her mother had been searching for Papa as early as October before her December death. A man in the nearby village of Bidarrai had gone missing in America like Papa, and had miraculously been found in Argentina. She wrote a letter, maybe several to the area where this man had been found, in desperate hope of some remote connection to Papa, but nothing — still nothing. While in the darkness of this story, without thinking, I blurted out how

Papa had been in a terrible car accident before even my sister was born, and how he had filed a lawsuit against the driver of the other car's insurance. He lost after seven years, in the September before the December he vanished. While this story may seem irrelevant to some, it has great meaning for the Basques. The Basques remember, they don't talk about failure. Many Basque men had come to the states to herd sheep, for two, three years, sometimes more, they would remain all alone, with just their sheep dog and their flock in the mountain ranges of the wild, expansive American West. Some went crazy in those mountains all alone. Many never spoke of it again. Others made it down the mountain but found life too hard, too different from the village they knew growing up. Some lost money, their American dreams destroyed, and some didn't even lose money but didn't' make as much as they thought they should. All of them, I'm sure, were too proud; better to escape than face the unimaginable — failure.

Many did succeed and I have friends whose parents were part of the two hundred plus Basque men from San Francisco who combed the hills above Lake County in the dark, cold of winter to look for Papa. I begin to tell Jeanine about the dream I had of Papa caught between two worlds, taken directly from my journal October 6, 2000.

I had a vivid dream just before I woke this morning. I told a bus driver my Papa had been shot. She was taking us over a bridge of water into a side of a mountain. Inside the mountain there was a door. An old man answered. I could see different people scattered inside this mountain and it was scary and dark. I told myself not to be afraid and that I had to go inside. I forced myself in and walked up a staircase that curved at the top into a balcony. There I saw a big white bird-like cage. The man asked me who I was here for and what was my name. I said I'm here for my father Beñat or Bernard Orpustan and I am Denise Orpustan.

He looked into the cage and called out my father's Basque name — Beñat Orpustan and said, "Denise is here to see you." I couldn't see inside the cage. There was only a spirit, no body. I could hear a very distant mumble — just when he started to talk the alarm rang. *He is caught between two worlds!*

What does that mean? Is he angry? Why was he in the cage? Is he trapped inside the mountain? Breath-peace-prayer . . .

I turned on the light and it shattered and became dark, chills — I stood with them — fear — it is gone.

I embrace this dream as a gift from the spirits. Thank you for this blessing." Almost a year after I had this dream I would find clarity and understanding on exactly what it meant. The following experience from my trip to the Basque Country in the summer of 2001 describes how the ancestors connect with the living when there is a need for balance, acceptance, and above all, for the truth to be known.

I told Jeanine that it was possible that one that October before her mother's death, she came to believe that Papa had committed suicide. All the arrows pointed to that — his mysterious disappearance in the hills, a very common method of suicide for the Basques. Maybe she even knew about his lawsuit and the case he lost at the California Supreme Court, the one I found, just by chance, on the Internet more than ten years previously. Maybe she even spoke with the same attorney from San Francisco that I did, who told her that Papa owed her a lot of money and she never got paid. Maybe, the thought of him taking his own life was enough for her to take her own.

Then, I stopped walking. I stood facing the south as the wind from the sea brushed across my face.

"Jeanine," I said, calm and firm, "I, we, will never know for sure, what happened to Papa. It is a mystery and this mystery has taken me on a journey to the deepest darkest places in my mind and soul, and has opened me up to the greatest joys and wonders as well. If it wasn't for this Mystery, I wouldn't be here right now. I wouldn't have forged the strong relationship with my mentor. I wouldn't have searched for answers about Papa, his culture, the Basque spirit, the ancient mystical ways of our ancestors, if it wasn't for his disappearance. In many ways, as strange it sounds, I'm not sure that life could have un-folded any other way than it has."

I want to know him, his character, his life, and the stories of his youth, like the one my aunt Marie Jeanne told years ago about him at sixteen or seventeen years of age, hunting and falling into a water hole because he couldn't take his eyes off the birds in the sky. Everything in his sake had gotten wet. He returned to the house with nothing but a bag of water. He loved nature, so much that every waking moment he wasn't working, eating, or sleeping, he was there. I can only imagine him, walking through the thick oak, pine, and manzanita forests above Clearlake, with his long, lean, tan legs, and deep, dark beautiful Basque eyes. I can almost feel the pulse of excitement as he found a rabbit, quail, maybe a deer, and the joy he felt sharing a dinner later that evening, red wine in hand, with his friends. These are memories I want to pass on to Delaney and Beñat, not lawsuits, lost money, and disappointments, not worries he never shared with anyone, as he counted his dollars every night after work. I want them to know the Papa held me on his lap, and smiled proudly as he looked down at me and my sister.

And most of all, I want to show my children that his death has taught me more about life than life itself. I have learned that it doesn't matter how people die; it matters how people live. That is the message I want my children to carry one their children. That live is worth living-do all that you can do. Don't ever give up on what matters most. Trust in your heart. Believe that there is something greater than even this life and that the

Great Mystery is beautiful. It is all around and within you. It, 'spirit,' 'God,' 'the ancestors,' they're always there beside you, holding you up when you think you can't stand any longer.

June 23, 2015

The sun did rise and the sun surely set as we strolled along the beach on our third and final evening in Hendaia. As we left the restaurant with family, having sipped sangrias and devoured plates of fresh fish from the sea, I noticed a canary bird perched in a round cage by the windowsill. The odd and beautiful aspect of this bird was that the top of the cage was open; the bird could fly away at any moment if it chose too-but it didn't. Instead, it looked around, up, down and gently swung from branch to branch. I stood there frozen in my tracks, as the rest of my cousins and their children laughed and talked, slowly meandering through way out of another four-hour dinner. I couldn't stop remembering the dream I had of Papa caught between two worlds. I also wondered how much Papa and I are like the canary. I recalled how canaries are placed in mind shafts for miners to know when the air is toxic. The canary will become sick and die before anything or anyone else. They are sensitive, smart, and strong in their own way, but because of their sensitivity they must take extra precaution to protect themselves from harm. The canary guards others because the canary feels things before others do.

    The next morning was horrible. I got the gastro or stomach flu, most likely from my friend's children who had it the week earlier. I couldn't muster the strength after being up all night to go to Gernika (Guernica) as I had planned; instead I drove back to Ortzaize by myself while the children spent the day on the Concha beach in Donostia-San Sebastián with my cousin Jeanine. I got lost, completely lost, on my way home.

Tired, sick, lost in France, not a fun experience, but I lived, as they say, and slept it off.

Alone in my bed, the shutters closed in the middle of the day, one could sleep forever, quiet in the village, no sound but the birds and sheep and cowbells. When I awoke from my long and much needed nap, I thought about how I had missed my alone time being here on this trip. Although I certainly didn't want the gastro illness, I was thankful I didn't push myself, but instead listened to my body when it needed rest. Perhaps it's my Basque character or perhaps my genetic makeup, but I can work. I can work long hours and push myself to unhealthy limits. By seeing how my children view me, my mood, my behavior, is a constant mirroring back of myself. I've let myself be silly again, like a child, laughing for hours over nothing at all. By just being here with them, in some ways, I've relived a part of my childhood. I grew up fast, had to be responsible fast, had to learn the way of the world fast, but here, life is slow. Within the slowness of daily life, I've noticed things like birds that don't leave their cage even when given the opportunity because they feel safe in their home, knowing there is always a way out to be free.

Sunset from the beach in Hendaia

Lesson 6

Don't keep searching for what isn't there. Be grateful for what is in your life. Magic and mystery are hidden beneath the obvious of everyday activities. The mystical path is your path unfolding in everything you feel, say, think, and do; in the choices you make and the actions you take. (Mysticism is the space between what is seen in Nature and what is unseen. It is where the spirit world meets the physical world.)

> "Among indigenous cultures, the Healer supports the principle of *paying attention to what has heart and meaning. Healers in all major traditions recognize that the power of love is the most potent healing force available to all human beings.*"
> — *Angeles Arrien,* **The Four-Fold Way**

What this is means is that nature is always sending messages to you within these spaces, within the light of day and the dark of night, between what we see in the upper world (the home and land) and what we feel is the underworld (our intuition, our connection with ancestor spirits). When dreams come to life in the light of day in synchronistic events, pay attention. That is nature speaking to you in a mystical way. For example, the dream I had of Papa asking me why I was still looking for him about six months before I took this trip was perplexing to me at the time. Yet, months later, when I was listening to Delaney read to me out of the Basque book on folklore she had picked out at the bookstore in Donibane Garazi about communicating with the ancestors, I knew what message Papa was trying to convey in the dream. He was trying to tell me to stop searching for what isn't my life and be grateful for what is beautiful, right in front of my eyes.

The Way of Two Worlds is to let go of the past (physical world), hold on to the present (between two worlds) and believe in the future (spiritual world). Have trust, faith, patience and tenacity to integrate teachings by noticing signs and messages. Harvest your life dream through creative expressions and you will see the fruits of your labor.

Your dreams will manifest in time.

7
The Way of the Universe

"Rarely do we realize that if we simply take time to marvel at life's gifts and give thanks for them, we activate stunning opportunities to increase their influence in our lives."
— Angeles Arrien, *Living in Gratitude*

Our last day in Ortzaize, I woke up early and cleaned our vacation rental; not the kind of cleaning my Basque female relatives and friends do, the kind I do in California. The women here clean with toothbrushes, leaving no trace of dirt or dust anywhere. I tend to "pick up the clutter" and get the dust balls off the floor. Let's just say, I paid the extra sixty euros for the cleaner to come in after me, and I'm sure the owners are grateful that I did. I had help though, from my good friend Diane. We became fast friends when we moved here in 2010. It's unbelievable we hadn't met until the Fête de Ortzaize here in the Basque Country when we must have crossed paths so many times in San Francisco. Three weeks after we shared a beer in the village square at the summer festival, she told me her father had searched for Papa. She had always heard about the story of this young man from Ortzaize disappeared in the hills above Lake County but it wasn't until we became friends, that she realized I was the little fifteen-month-old girl whose father went hunting and never came home. We became fast friends, almost sisters and to this day, I consider her and her parents' family.

The children and I packed out bags, pushing the maximum weight limit with our canned duck, pâté, and fois gras from Arnabar village store, the gifts of shirts and jewelry from my cousins, and the extra pair of espadrilles for home. Then, we made our rounds in village to say goodbye to my good friend Diane and her three children. Fortunately, we didn't really have to say goodbye because she was leaving soon for San Francisco to see her parents and was planning to visit us in Clearlake for a few days.

Door of Tipirena

Next, we drove out to my uncle's house, Tipirena — that three-story stone "falcon crest" with overgrown ivy, situated among my family's lush, green vineyard on the gentle slope of the base of the mountain range. He was waiting there, standing tall and proud at the doorway when we pulled up his windy driveway. We shared stories of our vacation out on his glass-encircled veranda, surrounded by his colorful pink, red, and yellow rose garden that didn't require watering. It rains every few days in the lowland valleys and the sun usually makes it way out in the summer, a perfect combination for vegetable and flower gardens.

Ariel view of Tipirena

We had a lovely, brief visit, much more relaxed and comfortable now that we have spent more time together, mostly from the two years we lived here and even spent Christmas Eve together, listening to choral music and watching the snow fall outside his window. When it was time to go, he walked us to the doorway, kissed both our cheeks as the French always do and watched us disappear down the driveway once again. Sometimes coming here feels like just hellos and goodbyes, marking the passage of time with each visit. This time, I saw something different in my uncle as we drove off. I looked back at his face and it had changed, but so had mine. I saw and felt a vulnerability and sadness, an empty heart, perhaps the same empty heart I will feel when you two leave the house for college. There is a special love we share for each other, my uncle and I, an unspoken one, a respectful one, and a bond that is joined and united by our common love of Papa, and perhaps even more than that, the enduring and supreme love that comes from having children of your own. He didn't have to say but for a flashing moment, his heart opened up and I could see, through his motionless stare, and his blushing cheeks, that he was missing us already, and we were feeling the same. I worried, as I think he did as well, that there might not be another visit. We had both learned through losing Papa that nothing in life is sure and uncertainty is the only certainty we can know.

Photos of family ancestors

Around seven that evening, the sun still shining bright from the long summer day, my cousin's son David, picked me up in his carpentry work van to go to the mill house. My uncle had arranged this meeting after he got my OK to move forward on the plan. David would visit the mill and give an estimate of what it would cost to pull the seven stone wheels from the bottom of the creek and then, finish the roof.

I had forgotten the key to the mill so David leapt up onto the lower part of the roof to peer inside the open mill. The main area of the mill was still exposed to the elements. Over time, the old roof had caved in and all that remained were falling debris of rotten wood and overgrown ivy, with rugged stones exposed at the edge. As we stood on the field together, gazing up at this monstrous mill house, still standing after all these years of neglect, through flood, rainstorm, snow and hail, he turned to me and said: "*Toute est possible*." My cousin Peio always said this to me, that "anything was possible." It was one of our code phrases for life is hard sometimes but don't give up. Without taking my eyes off the mill house, I said, "Peio always says that. I too believe, that anything is possible. Let's do it!" The seven massive heavy stone, pebble, and cement wheels, over 350 years old, would be the hardest job. Lifting the wheels out would be tricky as the wall is high and the *manitou* (loader) will need to rise high enough and deep enough to move them from the creek bed to the field. I then, started to worry if it would be safe, if it would put anyone in danger, but David assured me that it was not dangerous and again, it was possible, anything was possible when it came to finally rebuilding Papa's mill house, the lost uncle from America with big dreams destroyed, cut short before his time had come.

I could see in David's eyes that this was no ordinary job. He too had grown up hearing the story of Papa and watching his grandparents, my godparents, stare deep, dark and blank into the distance in moments of uncomfortable silence, sorrowful, empty silence, when his name was mentioned at the dinner table. During his childhood, he had heard many times, the story of Papa. David wanted to do this for me and Papa, but also to make his grandparents proud, as they had helped to raise he and his siblings through a difficult childhood. Again, the mill speaks, and each family member hears and knows a different story, but in the end, the journey is the same — to rebuild and restore a part of oneself, to heal from the past and start anew.

We slowly drove off in his work van, me still apologizing for forgetting the key; my mind was definitely on vacation! No problem, no problem, Denise, always trying to comfort and make things right. As we bumped along the tiny dirt driveway from the prairie to the main road, I couldn't help but noticing how much David had matured over the years into a kind, strong, and hardworking man. His brown hair had begun to recede above his forehead and his dark brown eyes were windows to his soul. For a flashing moment, as we said our goodbyes, as I opened the van door, I felt someone else was there — a thirty-one-year-old man, with a receding hair line and deep dark brown eyes, staring back at me, lovingly, admirably, as a father does to his precious daughter. As he drove off, this young man is the same age as my father when he died, physically related for sure to his great uncle, and sharing Papa's same love of the wild nature of this amazing place they both call home. For the first time in my life, I felt, no I knew, that Papa's mill house would be rebuilt. I knew that a village was behind me and they would see that it would happen. I had come here time and time again with the same dream, with your dream Papa, and finally, after all these years of listening,

All the children go then to their grandmother, one after the other, her Godson first, begging and crying, "Oh grandma dear a story, please, one of your finest" (**Haurrek oro orduan, Amaxoren gana lerro lerro doatza, seme' atxi lehena, lausengaka, oikuka: "Oi, Amatxi ona, ixtorio bat, othoi; zure pollitena."**)

the mill would live again, its walls would speak again, and we would finally come home.

When the children and I arrived at Irochbeheria, it was almost nine, just getting dark outside. Peio was standing outside the kitchen door of his parents' side of the house with his cell phone in hand. "I had your number on my cell phone, ready to speed dial Denise, and here you are!" he exclaimed in excitement at this moment of synchronicity. "Of course, Peio," I knew you were calling, I mused with a sheepish smile. We both grinned simultaneously, knowing that this type of perfect synchronicity is always a good sign.

Irochbeheria, the house of Papa's birth

I could see right away my family had been waiting for me. When I had first arrived here, I had told my cousin Peio and his father, my uncle and Godfather Jean-Pierre that I wanted to hear stories of Papa for my book. I wanted to know more about his life and his love of the wild nature. At the time I told them this, we were seated outside on the picnic table drinking an aperitif in the sweltering summer sun. They didn't respond verbally, but I could tell with their eyes they both heard me.

When we entered Irochbeheria, the table was already prepared with glasses for drinks. My aunt positioned at the chestnut credenza opening the bottles of beer, wine, and whisky, while asking each of us what we wanted to drink as she lifted a glass in her hand. As we sat around the end of the table, in front of the fireplace and the window that opened to the street, I felt both calm and excited. I was calm knowing that my father was taking care of me, protecting me, making sure that I had all the stories I needed to take back home with me to write this book. Even in their busy lives as farmers, working from sun up to down, herding cattle and sheep, and pruning their vineyard to be ready for harvest, they were thinking and caring for me. This collective family and community sense of protection is unlike anything I've ever known or experienced in my life growing up in California. When you're not looking, they are; when you're paying attention to the subtle, unspoken messages and signs from nature, the synchronistic omens of predialed cell phones, they are.

My cousin Peio was the first to start sharing stories of Papa. He was just a boy of 6 when he last saw my father. Papa, my mother and my older sister Michele, just 6 months, had come back home to Irochbeheria for vacation. It would be the last time any of his family would see him again, including his late mother, my Amatchi. Peio holds his whiskey, gazing into my eyes, with a bright smile of anticipation on his face. "When I was just six years old, I wanted to trap fish with my uncle (*osaba*) Beñat but he told me I was too young, not old enough to trap fish with him. I used to sit by the river and watch him trap his fish with his own bare hands! One day, I pleaded with him to go fishing with him but still, I was too little. I threw fits, crying and begging to go but he just stared at me, with that blank Basque stare, and walked out the kitchen door."

Then, my aunt and Godmother Marie Jeanne tells a story I have heard before but relish hearing again, especially now, here at this moment, with my two children listening intently, in French, to each gaze, each word, each pause between stories. "I was working in the kitchen and Beñat, probably sixteen or seventeen, had just come home from school. It was fall and he walking home from school from the center of the village at St. Michel's Catholic School to the farm. He crossed a little river and immediately became distracted by the *palombe* (wood pigeon) and had to stop and catch them. Looking up intently, he tried with all his might to trap the palombe flying over him, but instead his school bag dropped in the river and got all his papers from school and his supplies drenched in water! When he walked into the house, he was soaking and so were all of his things. I had to clean and dry his backpack, his pens, and his clothes. My mother, your Amatchi, was furious because back then, the mothers made the backpacks out of old pairs of jeans and used real feathers for the pens for school. But your father didn't care that she was made; he wanted those birds and they go away."

Marie Jeanne went on to talk about his love of nature and hunting, and how when he was here on that last vacation all he wanted to do was be outside fishing and hunting. He would leave early in the morning and come home late at night, never really leaving nature, spending all his extra time outside. Peio would follow him around, copying everything he did. Peio adds, "Even now, after all these years, I'm always curious and interested in the wild nature like your father, fishing and hunting. He loved nature and so do I." As they're talking, I hear the old traditional folk song in my head:

"White dove, white dove,
Tell me if you please,

> Where were you traveling,
> Your route so straight,
> Your heart at ease?
> From my country
> I departed with the thought
> of seeing Spain.
> I flew as far as the Pyrénées,
> there lost my pleasure
> And found pain."
> — Traditional folk song, in Robert Laxalt,
> *The Land of My Fathers*

Hearing these stories, I think how possible it is that Papa really did go back for that rabbit two nights before Christmas. Just like his hunt for the *palombe* bird, there lost my pleasure, and found pain.

Marie Jeanne stayed in the kitchen as we left, kissing both cheeks, wishing safe voyage ahead. Just as my Amatchi had done with when left her for the last time, she didn't leave her bedroom or even walked down the stairs to see us off. It was too hard. I remember, being just eight years old, on our first trip back here after we received seven years of back pay from social security when Papa was finally declared legally dead. I had run back into the house after we were all in the car to go to the airport, looking for Amatchi but she was nowhere to be found. As we drove off in the car, I remember my aunt telling me that was just tired, resting in her bedroom, but now, I knew that when she said goodbye to us, she was saying goodbye to Papa, again and again, over and over, endless uncertain goodbyes. That memory was too painful for her to bear.

For me, I had learned to say goodbye as much as I said hello in my life. I had no more pain inside, no more tears left to find. I had hiked Baigura, touched the cave of the sweating aint, that mysterious ancient Goddess Mari hidden in the hilltop of Bidarrai. I had waltzed with horse atop a mountain ridge, gazing upon the valley of Ortzaize, speckled with red roof tops, vineyards, sheep, cattle, and wild horses. I had cried when I felt hurt and misunderstood, and talked about my sadness after long walks in the solitude of nature. I had come back again to follow a dream, a dream that caught the attention of my beloved mentor Angeles, a dream that had funded this trip, this project, fueled by our mutual desire to share the ancient wisdoms of our homeland with the modern world — a dream that had begun with my father's immigration to California as a shepherd and a dream that threatened to vanish the night he disappeared. Yet despite the many stories of how Papa died, despite the endless grief of watching my mother suffer all those years, despite growing up poor in a rural town with no riches, not even a Basque family to ground me, I had found my way back here once again.

For me, giving up on writing this project means giving up on rebuilding the mill. And the dream of building Papa's mill house is not a dream and it is much more than just a house. The mill speaks about the promise of a new day, about the courage to face pain and endure it, to never give up on what you believe in, and stand up for these beliefs at all costs. The mill house is a dream that is both rooted in the ancient ways of the Basques and nourished by the freedoms from the new world. The message is that there is always a way out and always a way back. There is always a solution to every problem, the most difficult being the decision to live again when faced with insurmountable obstacles and enduring grief.

I have learned a lot from my father and yet I never knew him. Because he died the way he did, in that mysterious way, it has allowed me to believe in mysteries, to see what is possible, to have the curiosity to explore every unchartered path, every opportunity that speaks to my passions and spirit. Most of all, this mystery has instilled in me a tenacious resolution to continue living, learning and loving — like a butterfly who has outgrown its cocoon, like the pain of the *palombe* bird who pricks itself one last time before falling to its death, singing, with pleasure, the most beautiful song ever heard. I've learned that Papa's mill house is about choosing life over death, about cherishing each moment in its perfect timing, each pebble, each stone, each stone wheel we pull out from the bottom of the river will be made beautiful, fresh, and new once again. The mill house is about following the river current and opening up to all that is possible, waiting downstream. It is about holding on to the ancient ways embedded in all of nature, while embracing the new life that is born.

For the first time in my life, I know the mill house will be rebuilt again because I have learned the most important lesson of all, from my mentor, my father, and the mill house itself,

It doesn't matter how we die; it matters how we live. The mill house speaks.

A road in Ortzaize

Lesson 7

Death and Life are inseparable. There is no end, just a continuous circle of openings and closings, new beginnings and transitions. Nature continually heals, renews, and regenerates itself. Feel and express gratitude for your journey and the abundance of blessings in all areas of your life. Be wise by giving and receiving love. This love is eternal. The stream of light and love is one continuous beam. Nature renews and regenerates as rich soils grow and new seeds are planted for future generations to follow their life dream. Follow the mystical path in everyday life to experience the blessings of life—health, life purpose, and passing on your legacy, a legacy that manifests in each moment through an alignment of mind, body, and spirit.

This is our best nature.

Appendix

The Seven Pathways Integration

○ Way of Wholeness (The Teacher)

Major Areas of Life and Their Meanings

Personal Development (Integrate spiritual and physical worlds)

Daily Life Actions (Sun)

Asking for what you want and need.

Inner Qualities/Character Development (Moon)

Hope and courage.

Life Lessons from Nature

Never give up on what you believe in. Believe in yourself as the self is tied to the family, home, earth and universe. Stand up and believe in something larger than yourself. (Nature is tenacious.)

Planting Cycles of Your Life Dream (Process) and Seasons

    Seeding the question(s) of your life (New Year and Candelmas/Imbolc).

Tools for Building Your Life Dream

    Journaling your dreams.

☩ Way of the Ancestors (The Teacher and Visionary)

Major Areas of Life and Their Meanings

    Relationship building with family, friends, ancestors, and community.

Daily Life Actions (Sun)

    Strengthen respectful connections to past and current relations, honoring both similarities and differences.

Inner Qualities/Character Development (Moon)

    Compassion and understanding.

Life Lessons from Nature

    Trust in the process and be patient. Balance action with reflection. Work hard but celebrate accomplishments, and take time for the dream of your life's work to evolve in the spaces between the activities of daily life. (Nature is unyielding and strong, but unpredictable.)

Planting Cycles of Your Life Dream (Process) and Seasons

    Sprouting your life dream (spring solstice).

Tools for Building Your Life Dream
> Sharing your life dreams (storytelling).

Way of the Home (The Visionary)

Major Areas of Life and Their Meanings
> Home Life as an integration of spiritual and physical worlds, a place of rest, work and play to nurture identity, and self-discovery of visions, goals and dreams.

Daily Life Actions (Sun)
> Nurturing yourself and others and discovering all sides to your place in this world.

Inner Qualities/Character Development (Moon)
> Honesty (truth telling) about who you are and what you need to nourish and discover your life dream.

Life Lessons from Nature
> You're never alone. (Nature is all around you, interconnected and interdependent.)

Planting Cycles of Your Life Dream (Process) and Seasons
> Growth and incubating your life dream. (May Day).

Tools for Building Your Life Dream
> Gatherings: meals, songs, celebrations, birth and death rituals.

☐ Way of the Land (Earth and Sky) (The Visionary and Warrior)

Major Areas of Life and Their Meanings

Work/Career as a reciprocal balanced relationship: sharing our unique gifts to others and the world.

Daily Life Actions (Sun)

Listen to what is needed in the world to regain balance, and caring enough to make it happen.

Inner Qualities/Character Development (Moon)

Peace and beauty.

Life Lessons from Nature

Focus on the positive, not the negative, and the positive will grow. See the best in yourself and others. Always be true to your voice, to your truth.

Planting Cycles of Your Life Dream (Process) and Seasons

Budding of new insights and illuminations (summer solstice).

Tools for Building Your Life Dream

Nature-based practices (farming, gardening, walking, hiking, and solitude outdoors).

Way of the Village (The Warrior)

Major Areas of Life and Their Meanings

Community as a central part of your life's meaning and purpose.

Daily Life Actions (Sun)

Give your gifts to those in your village and receive the gifts they bring.

Inner Qualities/Character Development (Moon)

Balance and harmony.

Life Lessons from Nature

Your dreams will manifest in time if you: (1) Never give up on what you believe in; (2) Trust in the process and be patient; (3) Realize you are never alone; and (4) Focus on the positive and the positive will grow.

Planting Cycles of Your Life Dream (Process) and Seasons

Flower (express) new insights and illuminations as they emerge. (Lammas.)

Tools for Building Your Life Dream

Creative expressions (art, music, dance, writing).

Way of Two Worlds — The Physical and Spiritual Worlds (The Warrior and Healer)

Major Areas of Life and Their Meanings

Life Transitions and Crossroads-Bridging and Times of Change-Uncertainty, Darkness and Stillness: Death of old ways as new intuitions and clarity emerges about your life dreams and gates open.

Daily Life Actions (Sun)

Letting go of the past (physical world), holding on to the present (between two worlds), and believing in the future (spiritual world).

Inner Qualities/Character Development (Moon)

Trust/faith, patience, tenacity.

Life Lessons from Nature

Don't keep searching for what isn't there. Be grateful for what is in your life. Magic and mystery are hidden beneath the obvious of everyday activities. The mystical path is your path unfolding in everything you feel, say, think, and do; in the choices you make and the actions you take.

Planting Cycles of Your Life Dream (Process) and Seasons

Harvest (manifesting your life dream through creative expressions (fruits of your labor). (Harvest and Halloween/Samhain.)

Tools for Building Your Life Dream

> Integrate Teachings and notice the signs and messages from physical and spiritual worlds.

Way of the Universe (The Healer)

Major Areas of Life and Their Meanings

> Blessings of Health: Life purpose and passing on your legacy manifests in each moment through alignment of mind, body, and spirit.

Daily Life Actions (Sun)

> Gratitude for your journey and the abundance of blessings in all areas of your life.

Inner Qualities/Character Development (Moon)

> Love and wisdom.

Life Lessons from Nature

> Death and Life are inseparable. There is no end, just a continuous circle of opening and closing, new beginning and transitions.

Planting Cycles of Your Life Dream (Process) and Seasons

> Renew and regenerate as rich soils grow new seeds (compost). New seeds are planted for future generations to follow their life dream. (winter solstice).

Tools for Building Your Life Dream

> Manifesting the Mystical in everyday life.

Endnotes

p. 10. "a type of payment or *ordain*": In Basque the –a ending on words is the article (*a*, *an*, and *the* are English equivalents). So commonly known Basque words such as *baserria* mean "the family farm," or "a family farm," not simply "family farm." The root noun is the word without the –a, so, in this example, *baserri*. The Basque article has thus been removed from Basque words in this book to maintain consistency of style with the English text.

"the spirit that gives it life": José Miguel de Barandiarán, *Selected Writings of José Miguel de Barandiarán*, 69.

p. 11. "candle gradually burned down": Ibid.

"by the ceremonies of women": Atlas Etnográfico de Vasconia, "Les Rites Funéraires en Pays Basque Nord ou Iparralde (Synthèse)," in *Ritos Funerarios en* Vasconia, 707–12.

"*argizaina* (guardian of light)": M. Duvert, "Dans quel context prend place la maison traditionnelle?," 21–26.

p. 12. "lighting the *kandelak*": William A. Douglass, *Death in Murelaga*, 32–33.

"resumption of normal activities": Ibid., 137.

"married female head-of-household": In standard ("Batua") Basque the word is *etxekoandre*. Basque is an extremely rich language in local dialects and usages, one of the things that makes it such a diverse and linguistically rich place. Batua Basque is a modern common Basque language that is now used in the school and university systems as well as in the Basque-language media. Throughout the book Batua variants have been included for reference.

"*kandela* on the *sépulture* of the deceased": Ibid., 139–44.

p. 13. "it eventually terminates altogether": Ibid.

"classic mass at the end of the year (*urte buruko meza*) still exists": Atlas Etnográfico de Vasconia, "Les Rites Funéraires en Pays Basque Nord ou Iparralde (Sinthese)," in *Ritos Funerarios en Vasconia*, 707–12.

"cared for the domestic animals": M. Duvert, "L'etxe entre le Ciel et la Terre-Mère." *La Maison Basque-Lauburu: dossier pour le jeune*, no 2 (1980): 70–75.

"women seem to have in their family house": Jacqueline S. Thursby, *Mother's Table, Father's Chair*, 29–30.

p. 16. "the *kostalde* is a place where the arts of life, good will, and enjoyment all take place": M. Duvert, "Dans quel context prend place la maison traditionnelle?" 21–26.

p. 21. "all beings converge and gather together": M. Duvert, "Dans quel context prend place la maison traditionnelle?" 21–26.

"quarters or *auzoak*": In Basque the –k and –ak endings mark the plural, what is generally –s or –es in English, so this is the plural form of *auzo*.

"seven villages for the whole year": Ibid.

"share the same geographic area": Angeles Arrien, The Basque People: A Syllabus and Integrated Outline.

p. 22. "that relations are maintained": M. Duvert, "Dans quel context prend place la maison traditionnelle?" 21–26.

p. 34. "the house and the funeral rituals": Jacqueline S. Thursby, *Mother's Table, Father's Chair*, 36–39.

"doilies and candlesticks can be changed": Atlas Etnográfico de Vasconia, "Les Rites Funéraires en Pays Basque Nord ou Iparralde (Sinthese)," in *Ritos Funerarios en Vasconia*, 707–12.

p. 35. "relative value and given circumstances": Ibid.

"was sort of a nun": Julio Caro Baroja, *The Basques*, 268–69.

p. 36. "specify the date of the funeral": Atlas Etnográfico de Vasconia, "Les Rites Funéraires en Pays Basque Nord ou Iparralde (Sinthese)," in *Ritos Funerarios en Vasconia*, 707–12.

"*ilhuntzian (iluntzean*, at dusk)": M. Duvert, "La Maison Basque, Un Espace Sacre." *Etxea ou La Maison Basque-Lauburu: dossier pour le jeune*, no. 2 (1980): 13–26.

"special fabric called '*hil mihisi*'": Atlas Etnográfico de Vasconia, "Les Rites Funéraires en Pays Basque Nord ou Iparralde (Sinthese)," in *Ritos Funerarios en Vasconia*, 707–12.

"symbols used at this time": Ibid.

p. 38. "first neighbors in a great circle": Ibid.

"cantor who relays the songs/chants": M. Duvert, "Dans quel context prend place la maison traditionnelle?" In *Journées du Patrimoine à Irissari*, 21–26.

"*hil bidia*, the road from the house that reunites it to the church": Atlas Etnográfico de Vasconia, "Les Rites Funéraires en Pays Basque Nord ou Iparralde (Sinthese)," in *Ritos Funerarios en Vasconia*, 707–12.

p. 40. "throughout Basque funeral practices": See William A. Douglass, *Death in Murelaga*, 209–211, for example.

"(the inhabitants of the home)": M. Duvert, "L'etxe entre le Ciel et la Terre-Mère." *La Maison Basque-Lauburu: dossier pour le jeune*, no 2 (1980): 70–75.

p. 41. "thrown during the daylight": Ibid.

"*andereen baratze* (literally "the women's vegetable garden")": M. Duvert, "La Maison Basque, Un Espace Sacre." *Etxea ou La Maison Basque-Lauburu: dossier pour le jeune*, no. 2 (1980): 13–26.

"cromlech and dolmen (Gentilbaratz, Mairubaratz)": Ibid.

"promises that they made to them": Ibid.

"they break the mirrors": Ibid.

"never turn one's back on them": Michael Everson, "Tenacity in Religion, Myth, and Folklore," 277–95.

p. 42. "protection of the house": M. Duvert, "La Maison Basque, Un Espace Sacre." *Etxea ou La Maison Basque-Lauburu: dossier pour le jeune*, no. 2 (1980): 13–26.

"rarely entered the church": Julio Caro Baroja, *The Basques*, 267.

p. 48. "the realm of the dead": William A. Douglass, *Death in Murelaga*, 209–211.

"or neighborhood before finally departing": Ibid.

"given to those who understand": M. Duvert, "La Maison Basque, Un Espace Sacre." *Etxea ou La Maison Basque-Lauburu: dossier pour le jeune*, no. 2 (1980): 13–26.

p. 49. "God will make an angel": Ibid.

"intermediaries between the living and the Deity": William A. Douglass, *Death in Murelaga*, 80–81.

"religious authorities actively oppose such beliefs": Ibid.

p. 50. "spirits will not come back again": Bullen, *The Country of Basque*.

"meeting place for the underworld": M. Duvert, "L'etxe entre le Ciel et la Terre-Mère." *La Maison Basque-Lauburu: dossier pour le jeune*, no 2 (1980): 70–75.

"'Our Big Father,' 'Our Little Father,' or 'White.'": M. Duvert, "La Maison Basque, Un Espace Sacre." *Etxea ou La Maison Basque-Lauburu: dossier pour le jeune*, no. 2 (1980): 13–26.

p. 51. "the shoulder under the clothes": Ibid.

"the ghost of burials": Ibid.

p. 52. "the construction and reconstruction": M. Duvert, "L'etxe entre le Ciel et la Terre-Mère." *La Maison Basque-Lauburu: dossier pour le jeune*, no 2 (1980): 70–75.

"the end of the sixteenth century": J. B. Orpustan, "Le nom des maisons basques peut-il nous renseigner sur leur ancienneté', c'est-a-dire sur l'epoque de leur première fondation?" *Journées du Patrimoine* (1994): 10–16.

"in Lower Navarre and in Navarre": M. Duvert, "L'etxe entre le Ciel et la Terre-Mère." *La Maison Basque-Lauburu: dossier pour le jeune*, no 2 (1980): 70–75.

p. 56. "common electrical or water supply system": Angeles Arrien, The Basque People: A Syllabus and Integrated Outline.

p. 58. "at mass (or saying it)": Julio Caro Baroja, *The Basques*, 279.

p. 61. "shepherds (*artzainak*) herd their flocks": M. Duvert, "Dans quel context prend place la maison traditionnelle?" In *Journées du Patrimoine à Irissari*, 21–26.

p. 63. "the opening of the natural cavities": M. Duvert, "La Maison Basque, Un Espace Sacre." *Etxea ou La Maison Basque-Lauburu: dossier pour le jeune*, no. 2 (1980): 13–26.

"the kitchen and in the entire house": Ibid.

"the day before Easter": Ibid.

"been many fires": M. Duvert, "L'etxe entre le Ciel et la Terre-Mère." *La Maison Basque-Lauburu: dossier pour le jeune*, no 2 (1980): 70–75.

p. 64. "they accomplish certain work": Ibid.

"the kitchen, as well as the Virgin": M. Duvert, "La Maison Basque, Un Espace Sacre." *Etxea ou La Maison Basque-Lauburu: dossier pour le jeune*, no. 2 (1980): 13–26.

"sky (stars, sun, moon, thunder, lightning, diverse plants)": Ibid.

"the sun is living": M. Duvert, "L'etxe entre le Ciel et la

Terre-Mère." *La Maison Basque-Lauburu: dossier pour le jeune*, no 2 (1980): 70–75.

"their journey through the sky": José Miguel de Barandiarán, *Selected Writings of José Miguel de Barandiarán*, 79.

"returning to the subterranean world": Ibid.

p. 65. "by the ancient Basques": Ibid., 114.

"short cut to the sun": M. Duvert, "La Maison Basque, Un Espace Sacre." *Etxea ou La Maison Basque-Lauburu: dossier pour le jeune*, no. 2 (1980): 13–26.

"stone on the doorsteps of the house": M. Duvert, "L'etxe entre le Ciel et la Terre-Mère." *La Maison Basque-Lauburu: dossier pour le jeune*, no 2 (1980): 70–75.

"cave of Zabalaitz (in the mountains of Aizkorri)": José Miguel de Barandiarán, *Selected Writings of José Miguel de Barandiarán*, 115.

p. 66. "means 'people from the sun'": Angeles Arrien, The Basque People: A Syllabus and Integrated Outline.

"lauburu (Basque cross)": M. Duvert, "L'etxe entre le Ciel et la Terre-Mère." *La Maison Basque-Lauburu: dossier pour le jeune*, no 2 (1980): 70–75.

"to the eye of God": M. Duvert, "La Maison Basque, Un Espace Sacre." *Etxea ou La Maison Basque-Lauburu: dossier pour le jeune*, no. 2 (1980): 13–26.

"personified by the Goddess Mari": M. Duvert, "L'etxe entre le Ciel et la Terre-Mère." *La Maison Basque-Lauburu: dossier pour le jeune*, no 2 (1980): 70–75.

"the sun is in the west": José Miguel de Barandiarán, *Selected Writings of José Miguel de Barandiarán*, 109.

"daughter of the earth": Ibid.

"sun on its yearly course": Ibid., 110–11.

"protect the house against lightning": Ibid., 112.

p. 67. "witches, disease, storm, and lightning": Ibid., 179.

"the mother of the moon is the earth": Ibid., 113.

"speak to you in the same way": Ibid.

"the moon (the calendar)": M. Duvert, "L'etxe entre le Ciel et la Terre-Mère." *La Maison Basque-Lauburu: dossier pour le jeune*, no 2 (1980): 70–75.

"moon is waxing or waning": José Miguel de Barandiarán, *Selected Writings of José Miguel de Barandiarán*, 113.

"the man of the night": M. Duvert, "La Maison Basque, Un Espace Sacre." *Etxea ou La Maison Basque-Lauburu: dossier pour le jeune*, no. 2 (1980): 13–26.

p. 68. "God, you give a good night": Ibid.

"according to legends from Bizkaia": José Miguel de Barandiarán, *Selected Writings of José Miguel de Barandiarán*, 112.

"related to spirits of the night": M. Duvert, "La Maison Basque, Un Espace Sacre." *Etxea ou La Maison Basque-Lauburu: dossier pour le jeune*, no. 2 (1980): 13–26.

"Basques for thousands of years": Suzan Erem, "Gods, Bears, Stones, and Stars." *Iowa Alumni Magazine* (Dec. 2000): 24–27.

"representing the North Star": Ibid.

p. 69. "sky with an uncommon understanding": Ibid.

"identical in areas hundred miles apart": Ibid.

"(Aquila flying along the milky way)": Ibid.

p. 70. "loyalty to one god and one church": Ibid.

"humans and their bear ancestors": Roslyn M. Frank, and Mikel Susperregi, *Conflicting Identities*.

"in the vision quest": Ibid.

p. 82. "to all collectivist, indigenous groups": Denise Orpustan-Love, "The Three Portals."

p. 83. "sixth to the tenth and eleventh centuries": See, for example, Julio Caro Baroja, *The Basques*; Rodney Gallop, *A Book of the Basques*, Mark Kurlansky, *A Basque History of the World*.

"Basque religion came to an end": José Miguel de Barandiarán, *Selected Writings of José Miguel de Barandiarán*, 117–18.

p. 84. "battle to conquer his circumstances": Robert Laxalt, "Land of the Ancient Basques." *National Geographic* 134, no. 2 (August 1968): 240–76.

p. 85. "shows up and chooses to be present": Angeles Arrien, *The Four-Fold Way*.

p. 86. "transporting wood to appropriate dwellings": Angeles Arrien, The Basque People.

"death and plans for the funeral": Ibid.

p. 90. "prehistoric goddess of death and regeneration": Marija Gimbutas, *The Living Goddesses*; Michael Everson, "Tenacity in Religion, Myth, and Folklore."

"and 'the woman'": Julio Caro Baroja, *The Basques*, 276.

"to those she manifested during the Neolithic": Marija Gimbutas, *The Living Goddesses*.

"Old European religion, as we can reconstruct it":

Michael Everson, "Tenacity in Religion, Myth, and Folklore."

"animal is sacred to her": Ibid.

"the goddess at caves": Marija Gimbutas, *The Living Goddesses*.

p. 91. "the burst of a fireball": José Miguel de Barandiarán, *View from the Witches Cave*.

"gold and precious stones": Julio Caro Baroja, *The Basques*, 277; Michael Everson, "Tenacity in Religion, Myth, and Folklore."

"palace of gold in her hands": José Miguel de Barandiarán, *Selected Writings of José Miguel de Barandiarán*, 96–97.

"the air by four horses": Ibid., 97.

"of formation, destruction, and reformation": Michael Everson, "Tenacity in Religion, Myth, and Folklore."

"in the cave of Aketegi": José Miguel de Barandiarán, *Selected Writings of José Miguel de Barandiarán*, 97.

"in Zegama (Cegama) and Oñati (Oñate)": Julio Caro Baroja, *The Basques*, 277.

"sky surrounded by fire": Ibid.

p. 92. "shooting out flames on all sides": Ibid.

"minerals resembling a human torso": José Miguel de Barandiarán, *Selected Writings of José Miguel de Barandiarán*, 97.

"to place every seven years": Ibid., 98–99.

"failure to give help to others": Michael Everson, "Tenacity in Religion, Myth, and Folklore."

"previous archeological sources could not provide": Marija Gimbutas, *The Living Goddesses*.

p. 93. "Mari having seven sons": José Miguel de Barandiarán, *Selected Writings of José Miguel de Barandiarán*, 99.

"the Basque Virgin Mary": Ibid., 100.

"the tail of a fish": Julio Caro Baroja, *The Basques*, 278.

"believed to keep their stones": José Miguel de Barandiarán, *Selected Writings of José Miguel de Barandiarán*, 127–28, n63.

"Basque little folk are always female": Michael Everson, "Tenacity in Religion, Myth, and Folklore."

"associated with birth and midwifery": José Miguel de Barandiarán, *Selected Writings of José Miguel de Barandiarán*, 129.

"power to restore social order": Elena A. Williams, "Basque Legends in Their Social Context," 107–28.

p. 94. "bread, milk, cider, corn, and bacon": José Miguel de Barandiarán, *Selected Writings of José Miguel de Barandiarán*, 129.

"the mother of the sun and moon": Ibid., 95–96.

"land is an immense surface": M. Duvert, "L'etxe entre le Ciel et la Terre-Mère." *La Maison Basque-Lauburu: dossier pour le jeune*, no 2 (1980): 70–75.

"grow just as living beings do": Michael Everson, "Tenacity in Religion, Myth, and Folklore."

"the caverns, the caves, and the abysses": M. Duvert, "L'etxe entre le Ciel et la Terre-Mère." *La Maison Basque-Lauburu: dossier pour le jeune*, no 2 (1980): 70–75.

"box text": Michael Everson, "Tenacity in Religion, Myth, and Folklore"; M. Duvert, "L'etxe entre le Ciel et la Terre-Mère." *La Maison Basque-Lauburu: dossier pour le jeune*, no 2 (1980): 70–75.

p. 95. "river, asking God for rain": Julio Caro Baroja, *The Basques*, 265.

"place of the force of earth": M. Duvert, "La Maison Basque, Un Espace Sacre." *Etxea ou La Maison Basque-Lauburu: dossier pour le jeune,* no. 2 (1980): 13–26.

"then, they are blessed": Ibid.
"the appearance of an animal": Ibid.
"the deceased and the divine": M. Duvert, "L'etxe entre le Ciel et la Terre-Mère." *La Maison Basque-Lauburu: dossier pour le jeune,* no 2 (1980): 70–75.

"ancient Basque spiritual tradition": M. Duvert, "La Maison Basque, Un Espace Sacre." *Etxea ou La Maison Basque-Lauburu: dossier pour le jeune,* no. 2 (1980): 13–26.

p. 102. "show up and choose to be present": Angeles Arrien, *The Four-Fold Way.*

p. 135. "the mantel in the kitchen": M. Duvert, "L'etxe entre le Ciel et la Terre-Mère." *La Maison Basque-Lauburu: dossier pour le jeune,* no 2 (1980): 70–75.

"ducts and in particular, the hearth": M. Duvert, "La Maison Basque, Un Espace Sacre." *Etxea ou La Maison Basque-Lauburu: dossier pour le jeune,* no. 2 (1980): 13–26.

"leaves this house, and all bad things": Ibid.

"the fire against the bad omens": Ibid.

"abysses, and in the houses": Ibid.

Bibliography

Arrien, Angeles. The Basque People: A Syllabus and Integrated Outline. Unpublished manuscript, Berkeley, CA, 1979.

———. *The Four-Fold Way: Walking the Paths of Warrior, Teacher, Healer and Visionary*. San Francisco, CA: HarperSanFrancisco, 1993.

———. *Living in Gratitude: A Journey That Will Change Your Life*. Boulder, Colorado: Sounds True, 2011.

Atlas Etnográfico de Vasconia. "Les Rites Funéraires en Pays Basque Nord ou Iparralde (Sinthese)." In *Ritos Funerarios en Vasconia*, 707–12. Atlas Etnográfico de Vasconia. Bilbao: Eusko Jaurlaritza, Ethniker Euskaherria, and Gobierno de Navarra, 1995.

Baroja, Julio Caro. *The Basques*. Reno: Center for Basque Studies, 2009.

Barandiarán, José Miguel de. *View from the Witches Cave*. Edited by Luis de Barandiarán. Reno: University of Nevada Press, 1991.

———. *Selected Writings of José Miguel de Barandiarán: Basque Prehistory and Ethnography*. Compiled and with an introduction by Jesús Altuna. Reno: Center for Basque Studies, 2007.

Bullen, Margaret L. *The Country of Basque*, third ed. Originally published as Orphipean. Iruñea-Pamplona: Pamiela (under the patronage of Udalbide), 2012.

Douglass, William A. *Death in Murelaga: Funeral Ritual in a Spanish Basque Village*. Seattle: University of Washington Press, 1973.

Duvert, M. "L'etxe entre le Ciel et la Terre-Mère." *La Maison Basque-Lauburu: dossier pour le jeune*, no 2 (1980): 70–75.

———."La Maison Basque, Un Espace Sacre." *Etxea ou La Maison Basque-Lauburu: dossier pour le jeune*, no. 2 (1980): 13–26.

———. "Dans quel context prend place la maison traditionnelle?" In *Journées du Patrimoine à Irissari*, 21–26. Second edition. Ustaritz, France: Institut Culturel Basque, 1994.

Erem, Suzan. "Gods, Bears, Stones, and Stars." *Iowa Alumni Magazine* (Dec. 2000): 24–27. Available at http://www.lastdraft.com/?p=13. Accessed August 28, 2017.

Everson, Michael. "Tenacity in Religion, Myth, and Folklore: The Neolithic Goddess of Old Europe Preserved in a Non-Indo-European Setting." *Journal of Indo-European Studies* 17, nos. 3, 4 (Fall/Winter 1989): 277–95.

Frank, Roslyn M. "Singing Duels and Social Solidarity: The Case of the Basque *Charivari*." In *Essays in Basque Social Anthropology and History*, 43–105. Edited by William A. Douglass. Reno: Basque Studies Program [Center for Basque Studies], 1989/

Frank, Roslyn M., and Mikel Susperregi. *Conflicting Identities: A Comparative Study of Non-Commensurate Root Metaphors in Basque and European Image Schemata*. London: Institute of Basque Studies, 2000.

Gimbutas, Marija. *The Living Goddesses*. Berkeley: University of California Press, 1999.
Gallop, Rodney. *A Book of the Basques*. Reno: University of Nevada Press, 1970.
Kurlansky, Mark. *The Basque History of the World*. New York: Penguin, 1999.
Laxalt, Robert. "Lonely Sentinels of the American West: Basque Sheepherders." *National Geographic* 129, no. 6 (June 1966): 870–88.
———. "Land of the Ancient Basques." *National Geographic* 134, no. 2 (August 1968): 240–76.
———. *The Land of My Fathers: A Son's Return to the Basque Country*. Reno: University of Nevada Press, 1972.
———. *In a Hundred Graves: A Basque Portrait*. Reno: University of Nevada Press, 1986.
———. *The Land of My Fathers: A Son's Return to the Basque Country*. Reno: University of Nevada Press, 2000.
Nevitt, C. "Lancre in Labour: An Analysis of the 1609 Witch Hunt in the Basque Country." *Journal of the Society of Basque Studies in America* 25 (2005).
Orpustan, J.-B. "Le nom des maisons basques peut-il nous renseigner sur leur ancienneté', c'est-a-dire sur l'epoque de leur première fondation?" *Journées du Patrimoine* (1994): 10–16.
Orpustan-Love, Denise. "The Three Portals: A Cross-Cultural Theory and Model for Social Work Practice." *International Journal of Interdisciplinary Organization Studies* 7, issue 3 (2013).
———. *An Exploration into Basque Spiritualism: A Heuristic Study*. Köln, Germany: Lambert Academic Publishing, 2009.
Ott, Sandra. *The Circle of Mountains: A Basque Shepherding Community*. Reno: University of Nevada Press, 1981.

Thursby, Jacqueline S. *Mother's Table, Father's Chair: Cultural Narratives of Basque American Women*. Logan: Utah State University Press, 1999.

Unamuno, Miguel. *Tragic Sense of Life*. New York, NY: Dover Publications, 1954.

Williams, Elena A. "Basque Legends in Their Social Context." In *Essays in Basque Social Anthropology and History*, 107–28. Edited by William A. Douglass. Reno: Basque Studies Program, 1999.

Ysursa, John. *Basque Dance*. Boise: Tamara Bibliography, 1995.

Denise Orpustan-Love, Ph.D., is a first generation Basque-American and college educator who lives with her husband and two children in Northern California, and spends summers in the Basque Country in Southwestern France.

www.ingramcontent.com/pod-product-compliance
Lightning Source LLC
Chambersburg PA
CBHW032255150426
43195CB00008BA/459